D0614893

"Myra Salzer has a vision of the awesome potential of each human soul. Her work has centered in helping inheritors find their real work. *Living Richly* empowers you to wisely conserve and grow your financial wealth. More importantly, it **gives you the 'how' for creating your personal plan for happiness, well-being and significance.** It is a must-read not just for inheritors but for those serving professionals who are looking for resources and processes to assist their clients."

> **– JOHN A WARNICK,** founder of Family Wealth Transitions and Solutions

"After reading *Living Richly,* I feel gratitude that this book isn't for me. Even though my dad is one of the richest men on the planet, the gifts he gave to me haven't been monetary, but rather have been gifts of ethics and values. **The inheritors in the book may have a more complicated path, and thankfully Salzer understands that.** A must read for inheritors whose challenges are beyond mine."

> **– PETER BUFFETT,** author of *Life Is What You Make It: Find Your Own Path to Fulfillment,* Emmy Award-winning composer, musician, and philanthropist

"I have just finished *Living Richly,* **a very thoughtful journey** through the thickets of our clients' worlds. Readers will experience an easy, poetic resonance with Salzer's informal style and rich messages. Dante would sing her praises and I would be in the choir."

> **– JAMES E. HUGHES,** author of *Family Wealth— Keeping It in the Family* and *Family: The Compact Among Generations*

"I found Salzer's book forthright, funny and engaging. It's a very easy read, and I discovered myself nodding in agreement with the individuals' stories. Inheritors can use this book towards a better understanding of where they are and how to live their life better. I think it is an excellent introduction to some, and a reminder to others, **of the human potential that gets covered up in the wealth process.**"

> – **ROBIN BORGLUM KENNEDY,** author (granddaughter of Mt. Rushmore sculptor, Gutzon Borglum)

"Inheritors are simultaneously envied, scorned, and courted not for who they truly are but for their special status and wealth. Myra Salzer has a gift for speaking to them in that rare and precious of voices—conversationally, at a human level, with humor and wisdom. Though *Living Richly* is, like all books, a monologue from author to reader, it works more like a dialogue between a caring coach and the fears, hopes, and questions it evokes in the reader as the pages unfold. Inheritors who read this book will find themselves talking to Myra from their hearts as she walks them through the process of embracing their wealth. She goes **beyond guidance to wisdom, beyond understanding to empathy, beyond encouragement to empowerment.** If you have been looking for a positive voice to offset the negative ones in your history or your advisors, *Living Richly* is it."

> – **JIM GRUBMAN, PhD,** nationally-recognized psychologist, consultant, trainer, and speaker; founder of Family Wealth Consulting

"The more years of valuable experience you have, the more you are able to distill the complex to concepts that are simple, accessible and yet profound. That is the triumph of *Living Richly*, as Myra Salzer crystallizes her years of experiences into a small gem for the reader. The book makes its case that **living richly is a journey for an inheritor based more on values and personal goals than on money itself.** It does so in an easy to read, conversational tone. As investment management is our forte, I was particularly impressed with the simplicity of the case made for low volatility investing. We struggle to make that case daily to investors, a case based on sustainable results rather than glamour and emotion. **This book will be a valuable resource to all large inheritors.**"

> – **TED SCHWARTZ, CFP®, AIF®,** portfolio manager, Capstone Investment Financial Group

"Bravo! For anyone lost in the confusion, fear, guilt or euphoria of a large financial inheritance, *Living Richly* provides a way forward—a way to reclaim or even reinvent your life. Where other authors barrage you with investment formulas or preach about how they think you should live, veteran wealth advisor Myra Salzer offers **illuminating advice and inspiring stories on how to use your inheritance to construct the unique and purposeful life you want.**"

> – **LARRY DRESSLER,** author of *Standing in the Fire* and *Consensus through Conversation;* founder of Blue Wing Consulting

LIVING RICHLY

SEIZING THE POTENTIAL OF INHERITED WEALTH

Myra Salzer

WITH GREG I. HAMILTON

The authors gratefully acknowledge permission to include the following quotations and lyrics (see also additional references cited at the end of the book):

- (p. 3) from *A Joseph Campbell Companion: Reflections on the Art of Living* by Joseph Campbell © 1993. Reprinted by permission of Joseph Campbell Foundation (jcf.org).
- (p. 45) "Once In a Lifetime"
  Words and music by David Byrne, Christopher Frantz, Jerry Harrison, Tina Weymouth and Brian Eno
  © 1980 WB Music Corp., E.G. Music Ltd., and Index Music, Inc.
  All rights on behalf of itself and Index Music, Inc. administered by WB Music Corp.
  All Rights for EG Music Ltd. in the United States and Canada administered by Universal Music – MGB Songs
  All Rights Reserved. International Copyright Secured. Used by Permission.
  Reprinted by permission of Hal Leonard Corporation and Alfred Music Publishing Co., Inc.
- (p. 48) "Galileo"
  Words and music by Emily Saliers
  © 1992 EMI Virgin Songs, Inc. and Godhap Music
  All rights controlled and administered by EMI Virgin Songs, Inc.
  All Rights Reserved. International Copyright Secured. Used by Permission.
  Reprinted by permission of Hal Leonard Corporation
- (p. 89) from "James Callaghan: The Statesman as CEO" by Alan M. Webber, Harvard Business Review, Nov-Dec 1986
- (p. 135) excerpts from pp. 10, 161 from *The Importance of Living* by Lin Yutang © 1995 by Lin Tai Yi and Hsiang Ju Lin. Reprinted by permission of HarperCollins Publishers
- (p. 140) from *Under Whose Shade: A Story of A Pioneer in the Swan River Valley of Manitoba* by Wes Henderson, Nepean (Ontario), 1986

Copyright ©2010 by Myra Salzer

All rights reserved.
Printed in the United States of America
First Edition

For information about permission to reproduce sections from this book, write to: Permissions, Legacy Publications, LLC dba L-Press, 1525 Spruce Street, Suite 300, Boulder, CO 80302

Manufacturing by Creative Print Solutions

Library of Congress Control Number: 2010931887
2 4 6 8 9 7 5 3 1

Legacy Publications, LLC
Boulder, CO

www.living-richly.com

*This book is dedicated to all
who seek to align their self-worth
with their net worth.*

*And to all my clients
who have set forth
on that very journey.*

LIVING **RICHLY**

SEIZING THE POTENTIAL OF INHERITED WEALTH

Table of Contents

6 Your Plan, Your Life, Your Legacy

7 Inheritance for Life (Seizing Your Potential)

ACKNOWLEDGEMENTS

Every inheritor I've been privileged to meet, coach, befriend, learn from, and work with has made this book possible. They've turned their own pain into power. They've turned challenges into action. They've turned obstacles into powerful life experiences. Each one of them serves as a fine example of how you can shape the burden of wealth into the potential for greater worth. Over the past quarter century it's my clients who have taught me these principles, instead of the other way around.

This book is the result of four years working with my co-author, Greg Hamilton. His enthusiasm throughout the whole process made it an unexpected delight. My business partner, Steve, and my co-workers and colleagues: Barbara, Melissa, Raquel, Brian, Walter, Mark, Jason, Alan, Russ, and Annie—all of them make a habit of bringing out the best in me. They prove an axiom I share often: Together we are greater than the sum of our individual parts.

My father, John, taught me resilience; my mother, Eva, optimism. My husband, Vince Cleeves, the foundation and love of my life, taught me that unconditional love truly exists. My grown daughters, Jessica and Michelle, very much their own people, have always known better than to take me too seriously. I join them in that sentiment, and perhaps after reading this book you will too!

LIVING RICHLY

SEIZING THE POTENTIAL OF INHERITED WEALTH

Money, Myth, Soul, and Work

We must let go of the life we have planned, so as to accept the one that is waiting for us.

JOSEPH CAMPBELL

Defying Defiance and the Power of Myth

I nearly named this book *Defying the Inheritance Myth,* but Greg, my trusty co-writer, suggested that was a double negative. "Your approach is so much more positive and constructive than that," he said. "Set aside for now what you are defying and *de*constructing. What is it you are *constructing* for your clients and readers?"

I stewed on that for many nights. But defiance, I thought, can be such an empowering action, like Rosa Parks sitting in the front of that bus in 1955 Montgomery. The odds are stacked against inheritors: Studies have shown that 70 percent of family wealth transitions fail.[1] Aren't I constructing a positive thing by working with inheritors to beat those odds?

And myths–can't those be good, too? Like the contemporary philosopher Joseph Campbell said, cultural myths have a power and influence over all societies on earth: every country, every tribe, every person. But Greg was right about this: The myths that concern me aren't the positive ones. They are the flawed assumptions, the ones that divert us from our true happiness and higher callings. Especially for inheritors, the rarely questioned myths of "money is success," "get yours while you can," and dozens more are, if you ask me, evil. I *do* want to tear those myths down, stomp them into the ground, *and grow them into something more wholesome.*

I'm a fighter. I don't take kindly to unhealthy attitudes and entrenched bad habits. But as I came to realize in writing this book, this fire comes from my need to protect something dear to me. My love of people pursuing lives with meaning, my admiration for those who reach fulfillment and then create more of it–these are much stronger than my aversion to the myths that hinder us. And so I will work toward harnessing this greater strength: I will work toward replacing the old myths with a new understanding.

---

[1] This is based on a study of more than 3,000 families. Though family estate transitions are just one form of inheritance, I'd argue that the failure rates are even higher without the structure of a family. We'll get into this a bit more later, or you can read a synopsis of the study (Williams & Preisser's *Preparing Heirs*) in the "Further Resources" section at the back.

Money Is Water? But with a Soul?

I'm not the first one working toward this sort of understanding—and positive action plan—for wealth. Some wonderful thinkers and compassionate humans have devoted their lives to transforming our relationship to money. Lynne Twist, author of *The Soul of Money,* makes an extremely compelling case for changing our perceptions of wealth, scarcity, and accumulation. She contends that we're wrong when we think resources (including money) are scarce in the world. She says that money is like water: It can flow **through us and carry our highest intentions forth to the** world. If you read her book and aren't inspired to seek what she calls the "highest use of your resources," then, well, *I have words for you.*

Twist makes her case so well that I disclose it up front and vow I'll not try to outdo her. In fact I hope to take the concepts she presents so eloquently, at least the ones that are relevant to inheritors, and put them to work for you. That's my thing: I'm less a philosopher and more a doer.

Dreams Take Work
(You Don't Get to Sleep Through Them!)

If you've got a dream in your sights but can't figure out what's next, you're ready for this book. Before I let you soar away on your sky-high aspirations, I would be remiss if I didn't point out that these dreams of yours won't just make themselves real. Managing an inheritance—and your life as an inheritor—is work.

Still trying to pin down just exactly what your dreams and aspirations might be? If you haven't yet had a dream you'd make sacrifices for, I don't think you've searched deeply enough. I suppose it's possible that there are people out there with uninspiring dreams, but I doubt it. I'll spend a little time in these pages seeing if I can spark that investigation—but in the end, only you can tap into your core passions. And when you do, you'll discover the efforts—and even sacrifices—it may take to find your true callings are in fact investments in yourself and your potential. What greater return on investment (ROI: that holy grail sought by all businesses) could you possibly realize?

Luckily, the quest for your own personal grail need not be a lonely one. In a quarter century of working with inheritors, I've met some amazing individuals. What makes them most amazing is not their wealth, or even their life dreams, but their willingness to learn, grow, and collaborate to achieve those aspirations.

A worthy pair of companions on your adventure may just turn out to be the books of Mr. James E. Hughes. Hughes has, in my humble opinion, contributed more than any other advisor to the field of human-centered wealth management. His *Family Wealth* and its sequel are two of the most important works available to inheritors, families, and their advisors. These books seek to counteract the disturbing trend of failing wealth transitions.

I could go on about all the incredible resources out there for inheritors—and as a matter of fact, that's exactly what I intend to do in this book! So, if you do me the favor of finishing this little book, setting aside any dire sense of urgency about the decisions you might be facing right now, I'll promise to remind you at the end about all the "things to do" that may have popped up along the way.

In her book *Sudden Money,* Susan Bradley describes this time as a decision-free zone. She tells inheritors, those who are suddenly realizing the magnitude of their fortune, to give themselves several weeks, or even a few months, before making any decisions about their wealth: how to invest it, whether to share it with others, how big a spree to go on, where to run and hide from all of this. Other authors have proposed that you take six months to a year before you make significant financial decisions. You, of all people, can afford to take your sweet time.

My own particular specialty is in working with inheritors in the multimillion-dollar net worth range. At that level, you're approaching (or well above) the point of having enough to assure almost any lifestyle throughout your entire life. That doesn't mean you've "got it made," as we'll discuss extensively in this book, but you've got enough resources that you can take your time with the decisions you're facing. Within my approach, let's call this the "you can afford the time to make good decisions" rule, or the "don't panic" clause.

Here's my professional opinion about inheritance: It's a ton of work. You can't ignore this fact and you can't run from it. But you don't have to be buried by it, either. There are good people out there, with valuable resources at their disposal, who can help you in all that you're facing. That holds true no matter how personal, unprecedented, and convoluted your situation may seem to be. To get your arms around your wealth and make something healthy of it, you must take advantage of outside resources. You can look at it as outsourcing the drudgery of your wealth.

You Can, You Will, and You Might Even Enjoy It!

No matter where your money came from, no matter what confusion it brings, no matter what strings may be attached, as an inheritor your wealth is a fact of your life. Too many people say "must be nice," thinking you've got it made. Others are critical or jealous or just plain grumpy and say the odds are actually stacked against you and your wealth; they say temptation, laziness, greed, and a lack of purpose will bring you down. I fall somewhere in between: Inherited wealth need not be a loathsome burden, but it's also not an express train to enlightenment.

> *It's not only possible but necessary for you to manage your inheritance in ways that fulfill you as a human being.*

Like Lynne Twist, I think wealth can work like water: It can carry your highest ideals to the world. You can accomplish great and wonderful things in your lifetime and beyond. But to *have it made,* you've got to *make it yourself.* I'm not talking money here, I'm talking life.

My first piece of advice to all inheritors is to take care of yourself. More easily said than done, right? If this book can accomplish one thing, it will be to assure you that it's not only possible, but necessary, for you to manage your inheritance in ways that fulfill you as a human being. That starts with letting go of the things that are holding you back. Don't just pretend things will fix themselves: Learn what you'll require in order to wisely delegate duties that don't enrich your life, and take control of the things that matter.

We're not talking about getting rich, being rich, or staying rich—for inheritors at this level the bigger challenge is *living:* shedding all that's holding you back so you may live a life that is about fulfilling your greatest potential. There's a difference between being rich and living richly: I'm interested in inheritors who have aspirations, even if you're not sure you can articulate them. And I'm particularly fond of inheritors who have the gumption to go after those aspirations, even if you have no clue how.

That's where I believe I can help: I'm writing to give you enough **comfort** (Chapters 1–2) to ask the really important questions; to give you enough background **knowledge** (Chapters 3–4) to wisely recruit and qualify your team of advisors; to give you a **structure** (Chapters 5–6) from which you can manage your wealth—and your advisors—

without it becoming a full-time job; and finally to give you the **confidence** (Chapter 7) to dive out of your comfort zone and into the realm of your dreams. Shall we?

CHAPTER ONE

Net Worth vs. Self-Worth

*The word wealthy has its roots in well-being and is
meant to connote not only large amounts of money
but also a rich and satisfying life.*

LYNNE TWIST

Take Comfort ... and Leave It Behind

Seventy percent of wealth transitions fail. Oh wait, I was
going to start this book with something uplifting. Well,
darn, I blew it already. Too late to go back, I suppose.
Since it's out there, that 70 percent statistic came from a 2003
study of 3,250 wealthy families. The study's definition of failure, simplified, is when inheritors (those within one generation
of the source of wealth) lose control of their family's fortune.
Typically their family harmony disintegrates along with it.

Perhaps I'm being overly dramatic by focusing only on the failure rate. Let's take a glass-is-30-percent-full perspective and say that according to this and other studies, three in 10 wealth transitions *succeed*. Hmm, still not the optimistic outlook I was hoping for. Did you know that the odds were stacked against you so threateningly?

I'm not going to tell you how to live your life. You already know, even if you can't put words to it, even if you're not sure you trust what your heart and gut tell you. Perhaps you had your life all figured out and an inheritance came along and messed everything up. Or maybe you had no clue how to live your life and inheritance came along and seems to have saved you the trouble. Either way, windfall wealth descends like the proverbial stork. No matter how prepared you think you are, inheritance changes your life forever. I, for one, will not allow you to pretend otherwise.

There is plenty of money out there, and it's never really "ours."

I am not a drama queen or a Chicken Little. I'm not saying the sky is falling: It's just a stork, after all, descending out of the sky with a little package for you. Money, frankly, is not that big a deal. What I take from the money-is-like-water analogy is that we can add our own aroma (or odor) to the water as it flows around or through us, but in the end, it's going to wind up back in the ocean only to evaporate up, rain down, and continue the eternal hydrologic cycle. The point is that there is plenty of money out there, and it's never really "ours."

What is ours? Our bodies and minds, our spirits, hopes, and dreams. Let money, like water, refresh, replenish, and transport those things that are uniquely ours, and it is then that we discover the true wealth in money. These are points that Lynne Twist makes in her book; it's worth a read. In fact there are a lot of great books out there. In deference to you for choosing mine, I shall pay tribute to the others by applying their ideas to your situation.

OK, perhaps I have a few ideas and opinions of my own to contribute to the discussion. A crass friend once told me that opinions are like armpits: Everyone has them and most of them stink. All the books out there are full of these opinions, so how are you supposed to know which ones apply to your situation and which ones stink?

Inheritance Is Not for Readers
(but Wait, Don't Go Away!)

I have a business partner who loves to read books. Not the kind of books you and I like, but treacherously thick tomes on finance and the economy. I don't think these books, or even books of just about any type, were meant to be read by *everyone*. I think people write books about what they know—their little slice of reality and wisdom—and hope to share that with a small subset of the population who can then spread it to others.

My little slice of reality comes from the past quarter

century working with inheritors. In that time I've learned that inheritance is clouded in unhelpful myths and unexpected challenges. For many, perhaps even 70 percent (a number I believe only on my grouchiest days), inherited wealth becomes a staggering burden, an unfathomable mess, a royal pain in the you-know-what. And that's a shame.

Mind you, working one-on-one with inheritors and writing a book about my experiences are two very different things. For you, reading a book about all this versus consulting with a real human being should also be two distinct options. They can both have value. I wouldn't suggest anyone hire an advisor, for instance, without checking references and asking some intelligent questions (not always easy to come by in the field of finance). And I wouldn't trust a book to tell me how to live my life. So my goal is to keep this one short and sweet (as sweet as I can manage to be) and turn you loose to engage your own wisdom and passion.

This communication thing we do, it may have started around a campfire, spread through stick figures smudged onto cave walls, and never really got much more sophisticated than that. Heck, some people don't *read* anymore, unless it fits on a two-inch screen in 140 characters or fewer. And that's OK, because if you were to read every book out there that promises to clarify the confusing things in your life, you'd be up nights into the next millennium. By then it would all be out of date, and you'd be a few hundred years dead anyway.

I'm here to tell you it's OK that you don't read—thick financial stuff, I mean. The tools you need to manage an inheritance are mostly within you. And it *is* important to manage your inheritance because, although money still isn't the end-all, it does carry its own power. In most cultures this should be an easier analogy to grasp than the "money is water" thing. We have historically imbued money with a sense of power—from Old West train robbers to today's X-Prize incentives driving space exploration. The point is: money has the get-up-and-go of rocket fuel and the stopping power of an elephant gun. Bad analogy; we like elephants. But you see what I mean: It's tough to let go of the concept that money is power. So let's be real. Money *is* power.

Money Is Your Superpower

When was the last time you lay on your back, watched the clouds, and daydreamed about what superpower you'd like to have? Go ahead—this paragraph will be waiting when you return. Back when we—yes, hello again, caped crusader—back when we were kids, power wasn't a bad thing. We wanted to use it to walk through walls, fly through the air, or bake a 16-ton blueberry pie. (What? You never wanted to bake pies the size of swimming pools?) Back then, power wasn't always corrupting: It lit our dark nights. It defended freedom. It took us somewhere new and exciting.

If you think about all those heroic adventures, the superpower itself wasn't the point. Superman didn't get all uptight about how to fly better or more often, he just used the flying thing to, you know, pick up trains and girls and such. Actually it was mostly about Lois Lane ... and saving other people in trouble. Flying was just the line that connected those two points.

Speaking of connecting points, perhaps it's time to talk of something real, something so painfully real it's not even fun to make up analogies for it. I'll put it very simply: You've inherited enough money that you may never have to work for wages. You may not even know if this is true for you yet, and that's fine, but you've got a bunch of moolah, a chunk of change, countless fun tickets, and that gives you choices. Choices aren't fun. Decisions are. Choices are tugs-of-war. Decisions are when one team wins. So, as with any choice, to reach a decision you need to know your options. And it would be nice to know all the potential consequences (or at least the big ones).

Wise delegation: a sort of mantra for this book.

Take a whole lifetime to figure all that out and you'll realize you never had time to enjoy the decisions—the victories. Make decisions too hastily, or too naïvely, and you're likely to find yourself losing the tug-of-war. The middle path here is *wise delegation*; it's a sort of mantra for this book. Wisdom comes from study of books like this, consultation with trustworthy advisors, and your efforts to tap the innate intelligence that defines you as a person. Delegation is the tougher part—that's the letting go, the trusting in the knowledge and skill of other teammates, the participation in a larger community than just yourself.

Surround Yourself with Friends

You don't have to be a rugged individualist. The world today boasts many qualified experts and caring amateurs who can help you. To be fair, the world also boasts an abundance of conniving schemers and cheery incompetents who can lead you astray. That's why you must be wise in your delegation of the burdens you face. With a relatively simple system of checks and balances, you can avoid the conniving schemers (like, say, Bernie Madoff) of the world. Your own particular system of checks and balances is something you'll develop as you go, starting with all the guidance I can muster in the chapters that follow.

Before we meet some of the types of professionals who can help you on your journey, wouldn't it be nice to know a few folks who may have faced some of what's ahead for you? Here is an introduction to some inheritors I've worked with in various ways through the years. Take a moment to get acquainted: You'll follow Lance, Alysa, and Mary in the pages to come. They started out in different states of confusion, frustration, and anxiety. Perhaps you can relate to at least one of them.

✶ LANCE
Many Generations Deep and Still Swimming

A fifth generation inheritor, Lance was the latest in a long line of beneficiaries who were kept in the dark about their wealth. At the semiannual meetings of the family office, he and his fellow relatives were told to sign meeting minutes before the meeting had even begun. Financial documents couldn't leave the room, and the few questions that popped up were curtly dismissed with baffling financial or legal jargon.

The situation came to a head when Lance discovered one of the massive documents he'd never understood, but dutifully signed, had actually waived his own rights to claim *one full third* of his fortune. He searched for answers, only running into resistance from a "family" office that didn't employ a single family member. His 31 living relatives were beneficiaries of a long-standing fortune that was being controlled by virtual strangers. Odd.

At first Lance didn't know what rights he might have—and wasn't sure how to even find out. Eventually, as the intricacies of his financial picture became clearer, he didn't want to become buried in the tedium of wealth management, but refused to be shielded from it anymore. He wanted, wherever possible, to employ his rightful fortune toward his own goals. Easier said than done, it would seem.

❧ ALYSA
The Unlikely Family Leader

The only grandchild in her family, single and in her 30s, Alysa didn't exactly think of herself as leader material. Through college and all of her 20s, Alysa lived on a modest allowance of family money—deposited directly into her checking account—and had never seriously considered seeking a job. She casually dabbled in sports, travel, and playing her guitar. She spent time with friends. And she got mildly hooked for several years on one of those massive multiplayer videogames on the Internet.

Alysa, her mother, and her two aunts plus one uncle knew they were all due, eventually, to inherit the family's abundant but scattered real estate portfolio. Alysa's grandfather had purchased the properties over many years after emigrating from Greece. Known as Grand-Pappou, he was the family's only natural leader, but died when Alysa was much younger. That left his widow, Yia Yia, as the matriarch and de facto family leader.

Yia Yia bakes a marvelous baklava, spins spellbinding tales for her children with an impossibly thick accent, and knows very little about property management. At 90, she is an irreplaceable matriarch—but *must* be replaced as the family's business leader. As the estate currently stands, Yia Yia's untimely death would precipitate an avalanche of ugly paperwork and extremely costly (and unnecessary) tax payments for the family.

When Alysa's aunt, who was handling most of the property management for the family, fell on ill health and decided to retire, Alysa suddenly found herself in the role of leader. It was as if Auntie Cora had asked all volunteers to take one step forward and Alysa was the only one who didn't step *backward*. Alysa had never worked, had lived comfortably enough, and appreciated her leisure. Initially she had neither the skills nor the inclination to take all this on.

❀ MARY
Hid Her Wealth until It Couldn't Be Ignored

Born into significant wealth, Mary was also the product of a family with a strong tradition of charity work and volunteerism. She earned a graduate degree from an enviable university, and went to work immediately as a social worker for people from a very different walk of life: abused children in Chicago's inner city.

Unsure how to reconcile the reality of her financial circumstances with that of her colleagues and clients, she lived a sort of double life, keeping her wealth largely in hiding (even from her closest friends). Her siblings had a similar approach: Her sister, Edith, in Birmingham, drove a rusted-out pickup while overseeing the family's sizeable estate. Her brother, Alan, in New York, worked as a journalist and refused to let his co-workers see the huge house his wife had talked him into buying.

Mary persevered through her career as a social worker for many years until Edith—who had handled the family's finances ever since their father had died— was diagnosed with cancer. It appeared Mary would finally have to face the realities of her wealth.

In the very earliest stages of learning about her wealth, Mary came to realize that her piece of the family fortune was such that she could reasonably expect to have enough for a lifetime and more. With that came a new dilemma: So now what?

These people have been my clients, in one capacity or another, for years. Here and throughout this book I have liberally fictionalized their stories to protect their identities. I've selected them for details of their situations which seem relevant to most readers. If every inheritor's case were utterly unique, I would not be writing this book; you would need 100 percent personalized advice from a reliable pro. The truth is you do need a bunch of that kind of custom-tailored advice—every inheritor does. But, perhaps laughably, all humans seem to keep finding the same pitfalls—and inheritors are no exception. As funnyman Sam Levenson said: "You must learn from the mistakes of others. You can't possibly live long enough to make them all yourself."

Mary, Alysa, and Lance are on track to being part of the 30 percent of inheritors who remain in control of their wealth. Actually, they're evidence that it's possible to dis-prove (or change) that ominous number. If inheritors are willing to put in the effort to learn and grow, there's no reason to *ever* fail. All three of them are committed in their own particular ways to seizing their potential. They have found some answers to their questions, they have learned to intelligently enlist help in their journeys, and they have begun to create direction for their hopes and fuel for their dreams. Don't take my word for it: Their stories throughout this book will illustrate their progress and what we, together, have learned along the way.

I'm not about to pretend that one single solution worked for all three of these inheritors and I'm certainly not saying their work is done. For every situation, there are many pos-sible solutions; for every opportunity there are many tactics. Throughout this book you'll see how different strategies worked at different times and how each new challenge often requires learning a new skill or piece of knowledge. There are some general guiding principles that have helped Mary, Alysa, and Lance—and these same principles can help you, too—but wouldn't you prefer that the guiding principles of your wealth management be *your* principles? That's where I come in: I offer my experience on how best to engage others in pursuit of *your* highest aspirations. The process is just sprawling enough that you could use a sherpa, a trusted advisor, a coach.

A Personal Appeal

Much of my professional journey has turned out to be a very personal one. In assisting my inheritor clients through the stages of wealth and working with them toward a position of empowerment, I've almost always found myself caught up in the personal dynamics of life, family, passion, history, and vision.

Working with inheritors is not just about the material aspects of money or the mechanical details of a portfolio, a life spending plan, or even a legacy that will outlast a lifespan. On the contrary, it is a surprisingly complex and sometimes agonizingly introspective process. I say "agonizing" with the sort of affection normally reserved for the freakish masochistic set. That's because, in my life, soul searching is such a painfully beautiful process that it makes me want to burst. Sort of like the enigmatic Ricky Fitts in *American Beauty* when he said: "Sometimes there's so much beauty in the world I feel like I can't take it, like my heart's going to cave in."

In many ways, becoming a competent and inspired inheritor is one of the most painfully beautiful paths toward self-discovery and meaningful accomplishment in the world. My clients have shown me that inherited wealth impacts everything in your life, from relationships and career choices to your ability to grasp your truest essence and find your ultimate path to fulfillment.

These are lofty thoughts born of gritty experience. I have seen firsthand through my clients that wealth is not merely a gift that says, "Now you've got it made." Inheritance has the potential to atrophy your life dreams, lure you into disappointment or disaster, and steer you in exactly the opposite way of anything resembling success. I believe it's partly because there is such a focus in our culture on worth measured in terms of wealth—we express meaning too often through money—that it is hard not to be influenced by these unhealthy myths and habits.

During the past two decades I have met hundreds of inheritors with talents and abilities untapped, like great gifts still in their wrapping paper. In our years of working together, we have learned an important truth: Don't wait to tear into those gifts and put them to use. No matter how daunting the odds, the list of things to do, the daily pressures, the unpleasant discoveries seemingly at every turn, you do not have to settle for merely OK. You *can* integrate your net worth with your self-worth. Your wealth *can* become the vessel for your personal freedom, the medium through which you may accomplish your highest aspirations. That journey begins by tearing down some longstanding myths.

CHAPTER TWO

The Burden of Potential

Money does not change things, it just amplifies them.

YOURS TRULY, AS SPOKEN TO VIRTUALLY
EVERY INHERITOR I'VE EVER MET

A Special Class of Inheritors
(with Extra-Special Challenges)

There are so many myths, so many unhelpful assumptions about money in general (and inheritance
specifically), that to pick just one prevailing myth
is to oversimplify things. But I think it boils down to a
fundamental flaw in our thinking about money: We assume
wealth is scarce, and thus we try to "get ours while we can."
This flawed assumption, when aimed at inheritors, most
often translates to the all-too-common "must be nice to be

you" attitude. This creates a mix of jealousy and dismissal among those who don't truly understand the intricacies of inheritance. Unfortunately, this vast number of naïve folks includes friends, family members, and colleagues you don't exactly want to close out of your life. Even your closest confidants may have bought into the myth that inheritors are lucky stiffs who aren't like them.

I'm not saying, "Inheritors are people too; you're just like everyone else!" Inheritors have a unique set of challenges that requires a different set of skills and knowledge. The challenges are not merely monetary. For Mary, her money directly affected her romantic potential.

❂ MARY & DEVIN
Her Money Drove Him Away

Once upon a time, Mary had a soulful existence as a social worker. Her boyfriend at the time, Devin, ran a local Chicago soup kitchen and food bank and together they made a simple living serving others. Then one day Mary accidentally left her brokerage statement sitting open on the front table. Devin learned Mary had a net worth over $25 million and somehow just couldn't cope with that fact. He broke up with her.

Decades later—and still single—Mary attributes the failure of that long ago romance to the burden of her wealth, the guilt and shame of it all. For many years she asked herself how she could have been so stupid to leave the statement out; usually she never even bothered to open it.

Mary's slip up with the brokerage statement wasn't stupid, but it was evidence of the double life she was living. And while living rich and living *richly* might seem worlds apart, there's no reason to separate the two. Specifically, I do most of my work with people who have multimillion-dollar trusts and inheritances. Yes, that "multimillion-dollar" line is an arbitrary distinction, but in my estimation, it's a ballpark indicator that these particular inheritors have one significant difference in their situation: *Earned income has become financially insignificant.*

I must admit that wasn't the initial focus of my work, but as I worked with more and more clients, I realized that a whole new set of problems emerged for inheritors at this level. Far from "having it made," this special class of inheritor faced a wall of burdens and countless pitfalls on the path awaiting them. How could it be, I asked, that the wealthiest few—those with such high potential to accomplish whatever their heart desired—had so little guidance and instruction on how to navigate the choices in their lives? Aphorisms like "it's lonely at the top" tease the essence here but only hint at the lack of support, empathy, and *good* advice available to the upper tiers of inheritors.

Then statistical results began to emerge, like Williams and Preisser's ominous "70 percent failure" study in 2003.

Between these studies and my own client work, I realized the myths of inheritance were more pervasive than ever—and the realities far more disturbing than people think. This was especially bothersome for me because, in my opinion, wealth has a special potential. While I'm fond of people who want to use their wealth to fix the world's problems, I tend to look first within the inheritors themselves.

Anything you might want to achieve with your life starts by tapping into your innermost requirements. When your needs are met, everything else you do can bank on this abundant source of self-worth. From there you can find control of your wealth and put it to work for the things that will engage your heart and soul for the rest of your life. The collaboration of you and your money can be a partnership with fuel enough not just for your lifetime, but for your legacy. And off you go, speeding toward your own sunny destiny, leaving those specters of failure in the dust behind you.

Peachy stuff, huh? If only it were that easy. It's not rocket science, but it's not a cakewalk either. Let's call it a rocket-walk. Or cake science. I work with upper tiers of inheritors because 1) your potential is enormous and 2) I enjoy the challenge—of challenging you.

"Earned" Wealth and the Marionette's Dance

The finance industry is not known for wordsmiths or poet-warriors. Creating ever more obscure and confusing jargon is almost a source of pride in this field—a thinly veiled attempt by the worst of the television money analysts, for instance, to baffle viewers into thinking they know what they're talking about. For me, the greatest crime of all the finance industry's lame terminology is the term "unearned wealth." It's used by many industry insiders to convey the difference between money in the hands of its initial "wealth creator" as opposed to money that has been somehow passed along to others. I would like to introduce whoever coined that ugly, unhelpful term to a roomful of inheritors and ask the question, "Is your wealth *earned* or *unearned*?" You might as well go on to ask, "Is it deserved or undeserved?" And get ready to run.

The crime of the term is its disconnection. The truth is that inherited wealth *is* different from other windfalls (say winning a lottery), and different from the money you make at a job. But "earned" is not the point of difference. Ask, "Did you earn your wealth?" of anyone who views their money as rooted in their own convoluted family relations, anyone who suffered through the fallout of family business stress, anyone tied up in all the strings so often attached to inheritance. Whether through suffering, loyalty, patience, unconditional love, or the ambitions of loved ones, most inheritors have a relationship to their wealth that "earned" or "unearned" doesn't even begin to fathom.

Another crime of that term is more complex, but it is an underlying myth that both founds and confounds modern theories of wealth. "Earned wealth" objectifies wealth as a static thing that can be earned, owned, and kept. It is much more difficult to pin down than that. Wealth can be defined in many ways; it can include many things and non-things, like personal values and family traditions. And it changes. Specific to inheritance, there are distribution requirements such as those of a trust; there are stipulations of a will; there are tax implications based on ever-changing IRS codes; and none of this is to list the shifting personal factors that often loom the largest. Consider people I call the *bankrupt megarich*. Like them, you have a net worth long on zeros and commas, but it may have bankrupted your other sense of worth, the one defined by your happiness, vigor, quality of relationships, and sense of purpose.

As the inheritor, how do you feel about the original source of your wealth? Is it from a family business that beckons you now that you are its beneficiary? Is it from an industry you don't personally respect—say, you're a pacifist who discovers your wealth is rooted in weapons development? Or say, like the DeWolf family's current generation, you discover that your family fortune seems to have emerged from the slave trade.[2] Do you even know the source of your wealth, or what strings may be attached to it?

---

[2] A couple members of the DeWolf family embarked on a remarkable quest to face the realities of their wealth's past. They chronicled this experience in a book (*Inheriting the Trade*) and a film (*Traces of the Trade*).

Unraveling the strings that connect you to the source of your wealth can be a daunting task, but it's a necessary step if you are to forge an open, honest, effective relationship with your money. While the myths that other people carry about wealth are a significant drag on just about any inheritor, sometimes it is *an inheritor's own paranoia* that creates the nuisance. Consider, for instance, Mary's brother.

❀ MARY'S BROTHER
...And the Hidden Mansion

Like Mary, her brother Alan lived a double life: He was a "starving" magazine writer by day and resident of a multimillion dollar home by night. He took pride in his ability to see eye-to-eye with his fellow workers at the magazine and was always careful to keep the evidence of his family's wealth a secret.

The one time I met Alan, he showed me around town, sheepishly pointing out a city park named after his family. Eventually we ended up back at his home, where a curving driveway opened onto a lovely Victorian mansion worth many millions of dollars. He told me a story of how, much to his dismay, the reality of his wealth had once sneaked "out of the closet."

His wife, who had always had a taste for large houses, found her dream home—this historic Victorian. For years after buying it, Alan was careful not to include colleagues among the invitations to any sort of gathering at his home; he just couldn't imagine looking them in the eyes the next day if they knew that he wasn't a struggling journalist like the rest of them.

For his 40th birthday, his wife decided to throw a surprise party and—you guessed it—invited many of his coworkers. Inwardly horrified to see them all in his living room, Alan admitted he didn't expect any of them to respect him the next day. On the contrary, he said, there was no backlash and he even felt a deeper friendship with many coworkers who now knew a little more about their officemate.

No matter where you stand currently, by the time you have worked out a frank understanding of your connection to your money, I guarantee it will have become indisputably your own "earned" wealth.

Let's say you untangle all those strings and find some peace with your wealth right now. How will you feel about it as your life progresses? From your single years through prospects of having a partner and perhaps children, growing older, through shifting personal aspirations, changing demands on your time, and emerging visions of future legacies, your relationship with your wealth will be a lifelong dance. Depending on how many strings you discovered were attached to your wealth, this dance may feel like that of a marionette. In your own proprietary dance step—let's call it the Inheritor's Swing—I suggest you learn to take the lead.

And while you're at it, take some scissors to any of those strings you can manage to cut: It's your wealth now; you earned it just by the merit of being you. *And now vee dance zee Inheritor's Swing: and a-one and a-two and a-swing and a-dip. And a-one and a-two and a-swing and a-snip!*

Is it really that simple to earn this wealth of yours? Simple, yes; *easy*, not exactly. Peel away the layers of complexity, and an inheritance is a gift. Ignore the baggage, the strings, the financial checklists, and all you really need to do is accept the gift. If you ever get frustrated, confused, or overwhelmed by the complexity, I suggest picking whichever metaphor works best for you to understand what your inheritance is: a gift, a dance, a superpower, a—well, at this rate, you'll have dozens more metaphors to choose from before you finish this book. If your breathing becomes labored at any point in these pages, please remind yourself that inheritance is just a [insert your favorite metaphor]. Like stepping on your partner's toe, it's all OK as long as you keep moving to the music. And thus we can proceed into the steps that will make up your dance.

Fun with Numbers:
The 80/20 Rule Applied to the 30 Percent Who Succeed

Many fundraisers and salespeople use an "80/20" rule to prioritize their time. The concept is that the top 20 percent of your clients or prospects will provide as much as 80 percent of your revenue. And thus you should spend most of your time on that most promising 20 percent. Still with me? I know not everyone's into numbers. Simplified, it just means that a small number of things in your life affect the majority of your happiness. So prioritize, tend to the important things, and you'll be happy. Duh.

Except when it comes to the swirling options facing inheritors. How are you supposed to know which 20 percent of your priorities need your personal attention? Staying abreast of new tax laws, considering investment opportunities, reviewing insurance options, establishing a college fund—the list goes on. Just learning what a GRAT, a CRT, an IDGT, or an ILIT can do for you can turn your day into an alphabet soup of mysterious acronyms. Which of these things can be wisely delegated under your direction? And where do you learn the knowledge you'll need to orchestrate all this on a daily, monthly, annual, or lifetime basis (to say nothing of building an effective legacy that evolves and grows even *after* your lifetime)?

If you're starting to sense how as many as 70 percent of all inheritors simply throw up their hands at all this, now would be a good time to speak the mantra to yourself: Don't panic. We'll get you into that other 30 percent yet.

Another variation of the 80/20 rule comes from entrepreneurs. A theory in business school is that companies should only spend up to 20 percent of their time and effort on "liabilities" such as paying bills and servicing debts. The other 80 percent is for "asset growth" or increasing value, revenues, and profit. In his first book, Jay Hughes applies this concept to families of wealth, suggesting they be more forward-looking and progressive. When you view your situation as if it were in a corporate rivalry, imagine a "competitor" investing 80 percent of its time on bill-paying and debts, leaving only 20 percent for growth, adaptation to new opportunities, and planning for the future. You'd have a decided advantage if you flipped their ratio on its head in order to spend the majority of your time on the road ahead.[3]

I don't think the metaphor of corporate competition needs to be carried much further than that—and besides, I'll have a hoard of my own metaphors for you before we're done. Hopefully, though, you see the value of looking at your situation from many angles. I'm dispatching with discussions of competition and profitability—all that focus on accumulating money—because you're important not just for your money, but for the influence it can help you achieve in the world. Think of what you could accomplish with your wealth. It's common to first imagine the big plans: feeding the hungry, saving the planet, flying to the moon, or winning a Triple Crown. Those big ideas are OK, but think for a moment about what your wealth could accomplish a little closer to home, *in your own life.*

---

[3] If this entrepreneurial analogy is working for you, see the "Further Resources" section for Hughes' *Family Wealth* (particularly Chapter 8, p. 93).

Why Worry? There's Plenty of Money to Go Around

In my humble opinion, your wealth's most exciting benefit is its ability to lift you out of the morass of life's little drudgeries. For me, toilet scrubbing, tax return preparation, and arguments over money issues are three of life's drags that I've always been eager to leave to someone else. Money concerns, all those dinner-table squabbles over who gets what and where it goes, are one of the most common sources of stress and unhappiness in the world (inheritors included), and I think it stems from the belief that money is scarce.

This concept of scarcity is a tremendously unhelpful myth that sadly afflicts us all. And if there was ever someone who should be able to shed all those doggone worries about money, it would be people with funds enough to support themselves for a lifetime. The bitter irony, so thick you could cut it with a knife, is that money is usually the first worry lined up at the door of this class of inheritor.

I'm all for dispatching with those money worries. For the general populace, sure: nobody benefits from the arguments, pressures, and misunderstandings that come from a fear of scarcity. But for inheritors with many millions in net worth, or more, I've seen a surprisingly prevalent fear of scarcity. From driving beater cars that spend more time in the shop than on the road to elaborate time-intensive schemes to hide (or hoard) wealth from others,

The biggest change money has created in your life is potential.

there are a lot of wealthy people spending too much time and attention on money.

I'm not saying to ignore it. Like it or not, there is a power and responsibility that goes hand in hand with being a wealth holder. But when the people with that power and that responsibility seem to be struggling with the same day-to-day money fears that the rest of the world faces, I have to ask what they're missing. I look for signs of denial or fear or ignorance of their wealth, and it usually comes down to this bigger but more nebulous uncertainty that looms over a fortune of this size. It is a vast and shadowy figure, and I call it the burden of potential.

The Burden of Potential

Inheritance is a part of your life; it's a package deal. Money impacts everything you face, from relationships to career choices. It can be the inspiration for achievement or an obstacle to experiencing the very essence of life. If you can accept that dilemma (anything else, in my opinion, is denial), then the next question is "Now what?" The biggest change money has created in your life is *potential*. You now have at your disposal something that most people work nine to five most of their lives to achieve. Imagine 40 hours a week, with vacation and benefits, to spend on something other than the pursuit of a paycheck—or to spend on work *that you choose*. All that time and energy dedicated to something other than paying bills or increasing a nebulous concept called "net worth" ... think of the possibilities!

Some people love that idea: Possibilities are wide open spaces, and that can be exciting. In Japan, the word *heaven* means "infinite space" like the sky. Conversely, the word for hell translates as "no space"—a concept like a tiny prison cell. In a country where three generations often still live in a space smaller than many suburban American kitchens, the idea of elbow room sounds pretty heavenly.

Of course, that's not a universal sentiment. For many, wide open spaces seem lonely and desolate. Infinite possibility sounds like another decision to make without guidance. Imagine stopping in an unfamiliar area and asking for a road map, only to be pointed to a bumper sticker on a rack that reads: **"If you don't know where you're going, any road will take you there."** When your inheritance feels like that, like a crossroads with no street signs, I'd steer clear of bumper-sticker wisdom and instead go find people who've actually traveled these roads.

But first, as no Zen sage has ever said in exactly these words, the journey of a thousand steps starts by sitting down, tying your shoes, and figuring out how this fortune of yours got its start.

CHAPTER THREE

The Road to Now

Well, how did I get here? ...
This is not my beautiful house ...
This is not my beautiful wife
THE TALKING HEADS

Spinning Yarns: Is Your Family's Story the Same as Your Money's Story?

When we stop thinking of money—and wealth in general—as an object (something we simply have or do not have), then we're on the right track. When we accept that wealth has power, superpowers even, and that it flows through us and can carry our ideals into the world—we're still headed in the right direction—but perhaps things have gotten a little muddier. This is an opportune time, then, to slow down and get to the bottom of the stories surrounding our money.

In his first book, *Family Wealth: Keeping it in the Family*, Jay Hughes is particularly interested in the stories behind wealth. He argues that inheritor families need to articulate how they are different from other families: What is unique and special about this particular group of people who are connected by their wealth? Hughes, like me, has an unabashed preference for the human and intellectual components of wealth over its financial realities. We believe the human side is where you'll find your greatest capacity for both conservation and growth. And without a story, a common set of values, an identity, there will be no clear idea of what you're trying to conserve or grow.

This is not to say that a family's story can't evolve over time; in fact, *Family Wealth* insists that each generation consider itself the "first" generation, articulating the family vision, updating it if necessary, and agreeing to this common sense of identity. Whether you can clearly state it or not, your wealth has a story, a set of intentions and hopes, and a *past* as much as a future. Hughes and I are not Pollyannas; we're not pretending that every fortune has a *shining* past. Hughes points out, quite frankly, that some trusts are created more for the purpose of hoarding than for enriching the lives of those who come after. I've seen this myself in uncovering details of my clients' inherited fortunes—details which betrayed that many trust funds were essentially about keeping money from the taxman rather than sharing it with loved ones. Unearthing the story of your wealth can be, as Randy Travis often croons on AM radio across the high lonesome plains, "diggin' up bones."

Diggin' Up Bones

I recommend tracing back to the initial "wealth creator," the person (or people) who first crossed into the realm of "wealthy," from whom your money originally descended. Take the time and do the research to find out how your wealth got its start, how it grew, and how you're connected to the people who have held it before you.

There I go calling it an "it." It's hard not to think of wealth as an it; I'm as guilty as anyone. But "it" is so much more than that. For this exercise, begin with the simplest element of wealth to define, the quantifiable part: the money. If we trace where your money was initially earned and how it has changed hands to eventually reach yours, we can then start filling in the details of whether it showed up on your doorstep with any baggage. In composing your current story, it's not a bad exercise to inventory the baggage you're already packing. Like spring cleaning, see what's already there before you decide what to keep and what to toss.

Baggage can be emotional, legal, moral, or fraught with countless other dilemmas in many shapes and sizes. Imagine a tobacco fortune falling into the hands of a young inheritor whose parents died of lung cancer. That's a big elephant in a small room that everyone is afraid to talk about—and that elephant is sucking on a fat stogie and blowing smoke in the face of that poor inheritor. Won't someone please open a window?

Ponder that seeming oxymoron: *poor inheritor*. It's the core theme I'm chipping away at in this book, the sneering myth that inheritors have it made: "Must be nice to be you— poor little rich kid." Everyone has family baggage, personal problems to overcome, burdens of their own potential. As if life wasn't tough enough at times, it just doesn't seem fair that inheritance can amplify our troubles. Inheritors tend to face a larger magnitude of family pressures and a more cavernous lack of guidance in their lives than the next guy. Don't be daunted. The flipside of that coin is the increased potential you have, the spectacular opportunities to learn and experience tiers of life about which others can only dream.

Oh yeah, this ugly business of unearthing whatever skeletons arrived in that trunk along with your money—I suppose I've been delaying that a bit. I must steel myself for the experience. Of course there is a positive side to even the ugliest of revelations you might uncover in the tale of your money. The Indigo Girls harmonized it up as a karmic trade-off:

> *Then again it feels like some sort of inspiration*
> *To let the next life off the hook.*
> *She'll say: "Look what I had to overcome from my last life;*
> *I think I'll write a book."*

How many inheritors run from the source and meaning of their wealth because they refuse to take on the responsibilities of shepherding it? Too many. On the flipside, how many intra-family lawsuits hit the courts every year over disputed fortunes? Too many. How many inheritors annually sue the trustees of the funds meant to serve them? Way too many. I think these sad occurrences are the result of misplaced blame.

In the early stages of understanding your inheritance, it can feel as if middlemen—lawyers, trustees, or the taxman—swiped your birthday presents before you ever got to unwrap them. When did these people hijack *your* story? If you're outraged or feeling helpless in this way, I encourage you not to get mad; get even. Write your own story before somebody else writes it for you—capture the story of your wealth and make it your own. Choose your heroes and your battles. Don't want your story to be a comic book? Choose your love interest and the exotic setting. Romances not your thing? Choose your own adventure. Make it *your* story.

Even if you don't feel good about how your wealth was earned (or if others criticize you for the source of your wealth), it's not too late: It's your wealth now. Of course unearthing all the buried skeletons and atoning for the past can be a long and painful process. Don't forget that there are others who can help, people who call this their job. This can feel like a Hardy Boys book or a cheap detective novel and, well—heck, sometimes it is. Yes, I've actually hired gumshoes to get to the bottom of a client's convoluted family fortunes. And once the clue showed up in an old piece of furniture. Boy, doesn't that sound like the plot of a Nancy Drew mystery?

❋ **LANCE**

...And the Case of the Antique Desk

Early on, when Lance and I first began working together, getting answers out of his family office in Seattle was like pulling teeth from a tiger. But when Lance discovered he'd signed away the right to determine the fate of one third of his fortune, we were both determined to find out what else was rightfully his.

We ran up against tight lips and fierce opposition from the family office, and for years could only piece together scraps of details. You have to understand the amount of legal red tape that accompanies many trusts. It can be remarkably easy, for instance, for an unscrupulous or simply misguided family office to restrict information from the very people it was meant to benefit.

It wasn't until visiting the home of his deceased great uncle, Herbert, that Lance got his break. At the reading of the will, Lance discovered he was receiving an antique desk that had been in the family for generations. As if meant especially for him, a locked drawer of the desk contained letters between Herbert and Herbert's grandfather (the family's original patriarch and wealth creator).

Back in the '30s, Herbert was the favorite grandson. As he grew older and his grandfather composed his legacy, Herbert gained "inside info" through the letters about his grandfather's intentions. These were anecdotal—but very helpful—details that had never made it into all the official legalese of the trust documentation.

These letters shared Great Uncle Herbert's extensive knowledge on the nature and restrictions of the family's many interrelated trusts. Without this input, Lance and I would still be bumping up against closed doors and locked file cabinets at the family office. Now, at least, we have a blueprint of all that's there. Did I say it was like pulling a tiger's teeth? Now it's more like plucking that same tiger's nose hairs. Ask any zookeeper· That's progress.

A point to be made here is that the way a family deals with—and communicates about—its wealth is ingrained in the culture, the very fabric of that family. In Lance's case, family member after family member had accepted that the family office took care of them, and thus never questioned the integrity or intentions of those tending their wealth. Great Uncle Herbert had known his grandfather would be horrified to realize how powerful the family office had become—and how dependent and helpless the family members now were. He also knew that by the fifth generation—Lance's—nothing would have likely changed.

What we discovered, in unearthing this particular story, was that Lance's family office had grown a life of its own. It was as if the family members themselves—the very beneficiaries of the wealth—were merely a nuisance to the ambitions of the family office. Creating change in a long-standing situation like this, while not impossible, is very laborious. It can take many years—even generations—and requires significant coordination of many family members. Sounds like a little teamwork is called for here, right? Indeed: we'll revisit teamwork in Chapter 4.

Family Ties—and Knots and Unraveling Strands and ...

Most inheritors are connected to the source of their wealth through family ties: blood relations or the bonds of marriage and re-marriage. Even those of you who aren't connected to your wealth creator by family have *your own* family connections that become more important,

> *Understanding your place in the family plays an important role in your relationship with your inheritance.*

more influential, and, in some cases, more of a nuisance now that you are an inheritor. Thus, it's time to shake the family tree—or at least sketch it.

Draw a chart with the wealth creator at the top and work downward through each generation to you. Show anyone connected by family ties and anyone else who is a beneficiary of the money. You could spend weeks or months digging up your family history, but that's not the intent here. We just want to see the dynamics, the connections between people. Draw lines connecting two married people or parents with children. Break those lines to signify divorces. X out people who have died. Add new people into the picture through marriage or birth. As you do all this, you may start to sense the family dynamics: the connections, the disconnections, the "strings attached." This is an exercise that's as helpful for your advisors as it is for you. For instance, the following two inheritors discovered financial realities that their family trees helped to illustrate.

❦ ALYSA
The Loose Strands of Her Family Ties

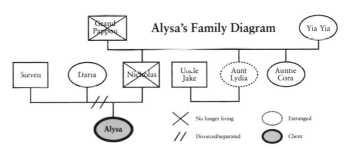

Hers was a seemingly simple family tree, but it revealed for us the likely generation-skipping tax consequences if Alysa were to receive money directly from her grandmother as planned. At the time, generation-skipping taxes were a particularly onerous liability on gifts to grandchildren. In 2010, the year this book is being published, that particular tax and some other aspects of estate taxes have been repealed (for one year only-they are likely to return with a vengeance). While the details are constantly changing, there are certain absolutes in estate planning, and revising Yia Yia's initial plan for Alysa's inheritance had many other benefits as well.

Alternately, if Yia Yia were to provide the gift to Alysa's mother, Daria, then it would raise the emotional question of whether Daria's sisters had received equitable gifts. That question was especially tricky as Alysa's estranged aunt, Lydia, was struggling with alcoholism, hadn't communicated productively with her mother or sisters in many years, and would likely have taken issue with uneven distribution of the family estate. Alysa's favorite aunt, Cora, meanwhile, had fallen ill and no longer wished to manage the rental properties that comprised most of her family's wealth. Uncertain of either aunt's exact wishes for her share of the estate, Alysa would be actively working with both, as well as her own mother and grandmother, to determine the best direction for the family's financial resources.

Her family diagram illustrated an overview of the people involved in the decisions Alysa would have to make fairly quickly. I warned her not to underestimate the challenges of coaxing responses, much less clear answers or decisions, out of far-flung family members (especially when one relative has become estranged from the rest of the family). Alysa studied the diagram and realized she would essentially be running a company with her mother and two aunts as partners. That's getting ahead of ourselves, but it's a tease of how valuable this exercise can be at both the early and later stages of managing your wealth.

❀ LANCE
Learns from His Elders

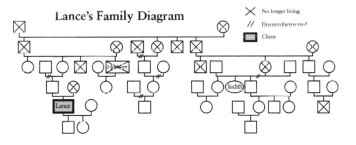

Lance comes from a complex family history, to be sure, but upon reviewing the details of his trust, Lance's blood relations helped clarify his place in the distribution of trust funds. For instance, consulting with a cousin (Judith) who was in the fourth generation allowed access to details of the trust's distribution timing that were not yet available to Lance's generation of beneficiaries. And locating the letters of Great Uncle Herbert provided even more detail and advice.

Through his relatives' own knowledge of the trust terms, Lance discovered he could expect forthcoming distributions that were large enough to notably affect his financials. Knowing they were coming within the next ten years allowed Lance to make current plans he wouldn't have otherwise considered: plans like raising his young children overseas for a year and upgrading to a larger house to accommodate his growing family.

Another takeaway of completing his family diagram included the cautionary tales he gleaned from the sheer number of premature deaths (from alcoholism or suicide) as well as divorces and troubled individuals among his relatives. He learned in our coaching sessions that his family's percentage of these sad occurrences were well above average, suggesting that the family's wealth had created more burden than potential for its beneficiaries.

Instead of allowing this news to dishearten him, Lance took it as a challenge, seeking to reverse the trend and use his wealth to live richly rather than being crushed under the pressure of it all.

Whether you take the bull by the horns, as Lance has chosen to do, or whether you engage a team to do so on your behalf (which is essentially Alysa's approach), this empowered transition into control of your wealth is an important step for any inheritor. Family dynamics can be some of the most resonant influences in our lives, but the variety between (and within) families can be staggering. Understanding your place in the nuclear and extended family plays an important role in your relationship with your inheritance.

Family Dynamics Can Be Child's Play

When creating family diagrams, I like to envision that I'm erecting one of those children's playsets with ramps for little wooden balls to roll down. When your diagram is fairly complete, imagine rolling that toy ball from the wealth creator down each generation's lines, and watch its progress. Observe the forks where one line splits into several and the "dead ends" where family ties end without extending to another generation.

Don't get caught up in the minutia of the diagram; for instance, don't spend weeks trying to find out exactly how Great Aunt Ethel died. The point is to get a big-picture idea of how many people are connected to this wealth of yours. Even if you feel like you have a good handle on the source of your money, there are always, inevitably, surprises in your wealth's history. Within the circles and squares on your own diagram, you may discover suicides, alcoholism, cancer, or people who lived to 100 years old. You may learn about entrepreneurs, philanthropists, families with many kids, individuals who never married, or people who married seven times.

Going back to imagining a little ball rolling down the

diagram, now imagine several balls of different colors. One represents money—make it green, perhaps—the financial value of your family's fortune. Roll that ball down the chart and see the places where some people added to it and where others may have taken from it. Now imagine another ball—this one representing values, ideals, the *story* of your family. (You pick the color for this ball.) Roll it down and notice how it moves among the marriages, divorces, children, and other dynamics of your chart.

This family tree exercise is a first step in answering key questions. "Where did my money come from?" "Did it show up with any baggage?" Unearthing your money's source can help you establish (or articulate) your own attitude toward your money. Is your money going in many directions or just one? Is it picking up momentum or slowing down? Do you respect and admire how it was created? Are you loyal to the principles upon which it was earned? Do you feel obligated to honor the intent of your benefactor(s)? Do you feel guilt, resentment, or confusion about the source of your wealth or its implications? Don't judge yourself, just be honest about how your wealth—and probing its origins—makes you feel.

An interesting side benefit of drawing your family diagram, and of seeing your connections to the source of your wealth, is that you have begun to visualize a larger network around your money. When you look back and see how wealth came to you, follow that momentum forward and imagine where it might be going into the future: *your* future. Consider that you are part of a larger network. That revelation has two important consequences: 1) you're not alone in this, and 2) your actions affect others. Someday a descendant or an organization might sketch a similar tree with you up there above them.

Who's the Star at the Top of the Tree?

You are! Forget about all that family stuff for a minute. Before your inheritance, there was a you who is still here (yes, hello). Under the inheritor you've become is an unchanged core, an essence of who you are and what you believe. This, more than your wealth, more than the obligations that others may be putting on you, is the true seed of what you'll be in your future.

It's so easy to get caught up in the financial to-do lists, the familial requests, the questions to ask, the answers to seek. An inheritor's load can seem heavier than the next guy's. When high-level businesspeople face seemingly insurmountable burdens, they often seek executive coaching. In those sessions they learn that letting the demands of their job override the needs of their own body and soul makes them robot slaves to an evil alien overlord. Same for you: If you let the weight of inherited wealth—all its promise, all its uncertainty, all its expectation, confusion, and tedium— take over the majority of your life, then you will have been vanquished by the spider race from Planet X. Fight back:

Defend your freedom and liberty!

Once again I digress. Forgive me. Executive coaching sessions are really nothing like that at all.

All I am saying (or was trying to say) is that in the effort to unearth the story of your money, don't lose sight of the story that was unfolding in your life before and outside of your wealth. Those foolish types who win the lottery, immediately quit their jobs, and suddenly change virtually everything about their lives—they are foolish not so much for this radical change, but for how long they had previously spent on a path they apparently despised. Many think their newfound wealth will forever change all that—and most ultimately discover that they're the same person they were, warts and all, before they were rich.

Look closely at the *you* that preceded your wealth, and tell me honestly if you despise that person enough to start from scratch? Of course not. How do we expect to make progress in this life if we don't build on what's come before? Ask any two-year-old how easy it is to topple a tower of blocks. *Crash!* It's when they learn to build them back up again that they have started to mature.

See? It's all just child's play. Except that to build the kind of towers that are within your potential as an inheritor, you're really going to need some help.

CHAPTER FOUR

Your Team

Ten Clowns Don't Make a Circus
THE TITLE OF A BOOK I SPOTTED ONCE
BUT NEVER READ

Envision This: You're a Leader Now

If you haven't thought of yourself as a leader before, you better start coming to terms with it. Leadership comes in many forms, and sometime in our lives (if not on a daily basis) we all must find the ability to listen, learn, think, decide, act, and *lead*. As an inheritor, not only are you forbidden to weasel out of this requirement, you must step up almost immediately.

Certain clocks begin ticking from the moment inheritors come into a fortune. Sometimes the stopwatch has already begun months or years earlier; sometimes before you were born. Stopwatch or time bomb? It's more like a stopwatch, but just for fun let's pretend it's a bomb.

Many inherited benefits have time limits, eligibility windows, and details that evolve (or vanish) over time. Federal law, for instance, has a set time period for accepting or disclaiming the benefits provided by a will. Most beneficiaries of trusts, as another example, have different levels of access to their funds as they reach certain ages. Remember how Lance unwittingly signed away his rights to a full third of his fortune? That was back when he turned 21, and it was a time-sensitive decision on which he didn't receive full disclosure from his family office.

An example that faces every inheritor is the array of tax questions that surround any wealth transfer. Tax benefits and liabilities vary with the tax codes, which can seem to change with the winds. Certain combined tax liabilities are now *over 70 percent* (as just one example of the variables), so failing to understand your tax options relatively quickly can drastically affect your financial picture (in ways with which only your friendly taxing authorities would be pleased).

Assuming you accept this urgency, defusing your own peculiar time bombs is going to require leadership. You might be tempted to jump in there like the movie hero and start clipping wires, but here's where the time-bomb ruse ends. Please recall my introduction's "don't panic" clause: You of all people can afford to take the time to get these decisions right. And that means becoming a leader.

When training firms consult with high-level business

leaders, one of the first required skills is the concept of vision or, more accurately, the ability to *envision*. The reason envisioning is so critical to leadership is the simple assumption that we all want to go somewhere interesting. If you don't want interest in your life, leadership is not required: Knock yourself out as the world's most accomplished couch potato. For the rest of us, interest comes from new experiences and curiosity about the unknown. Go marching into the unknown, and you better be packing either foolish bravado or leadership skills. The bravado angle may be fun for a while, but it's leadership—that calming, motivational influence of any great leader—that makes for exciting new experiences *that actually turn out well.*

That's why academic studies of successful leaders (and their admiring flocks) have identified "envisioning" as leadership skill No. 1. Envisioning is the ability to imagine a destination, a goal, an outcome that is not within plain sight. For people in motion, adventurers who actually chase after those visions, this has an interesting corollary: When you achieve your vision, it's time to envision something new, further out there, more interesting. So the envisioning task is never done.

That's an important realization. It utterly debunks all your hopes for an easy way out. Again, if you want easy, surf the couch. If you want to lead a more interesting, satisfying, regret-free life than that, then paddle out to the big waves: Step up and lead.

You're Not Alone—and You're Not *Entirely* Surrounded by Clowns and Criminals

The "ten clowns don't make a circus" line at the beginning of this chapter came from the cover of a book I saw for sale in a copy shop. I casually picked it up without any intention to buy it. It was a book about leadership, about division of labor and delegation for better teamwork. After placing my printing order, I looked over the clerk's shoulder at all the busy workers who were filling orders, tending machines, and generally hustling and bustling around the shop. Then I noticed a manager doing none of the above, not hustling *or* bustling. Actually, she was standing casually chatting to one of the other workers as if on coffee break.

I sat awaiting my order, skimming the back cover of *Ten Clowns*, when all of a sudden the shop's pace picked up. A delivery truck driver showed up looking for direction, a rush of new customers arrived with armloads of projects, and then the big laminating machine started smoking. That manager hopped into action, fielding questions from the adolescent running the laminating machine, directing the truck driver to another clerk who was stocking paper on shelves, and then stepping up to one of the cash registers to speed up the line of waiting customers. With *Clowns* book still in hand, I imagined what this particular circus would have been like without a ringmaster. Or what if there were only one employee to do it all?

Inheritance can seem like that: a ton of work, not much of it very interesting (no offense to the copy shop clerks out there), and not many people you trust to turn to. In an inheritor's world, there are many tasks with high stakes, countless complex details, and no gloriously simple answers for "what to do now?"

I never did read the clowns book. I think I have already established that I'm not really a believer in reading every book out there. There are people in my life who are better readers than I am—and I have made them part of my team. You, too, can form a team to handle the necessities in your life, freeing you up to accomplish the bigger stuff that you, and only you, care about.

You Need a Team

No matter how simple your life was before you got your arms around the scope of your wealth, there's no going back. Some people get by with $50 in software and a few hours to complete their taxes each year. Not you. Some people spend a grand total of one hour a month at the kitchen table to pay their bills. Wouldn't that be nice? A lot of people have relatively simple answers about what they own and what they owe. Bye-bye simplicity, hello complications. Alysa's situation may be more in line with what you're facing (whether you know it or not).

❧ ALYSA
...And the Prospect of a Family Partnership

When I started wealth coaching for Alysa, she had a relatively small portfolio. Gradually, over the years, we learned that she was due for a significant inheritance directly from her grandmother. As the estate initially stood—largely tied up in rental real estate properties— millions of dollars would have been burned unnecessarily in probate fees, appraisal costs, and other expenses across the properties' eight different home states. Since the titles to the properties were nearly all in Yia Yia's name, these costs—and frankly the sheer amount of red tape involved—would have been crushing.

One part of the solution came to light through Alysa's participation in my workshops and wealth coaching sessions over the years: a "family limited partnership." That family partnership would need a leader. With a better understanding of the personalities involved (thanks to her family diagrams—see page 53) and the specific interests of all family members, Alysa realized it was her calling to take that role. This was a valuable revelation for both Alysa and her family since, frankly, no one else was stepping up to the plate.

The financial benefits in her case were significant. She now earns a salary from the family partnership, thus shifting her grandmother's assets to the lower tax rates that apply to earned income. It's one way she's found to avoid the onerous generation-skipping taxes that she would have otherwise incurred (at the time—see page 53). The opportunity also gave Alysa a more compelling sense of purpose. In our years working together, she has admitted that she sees herself maturing out of those youthful years of video games, sleeping late, and seeking nothing but leisure time with friends.

In the early stages of her new role, however, she faced a confusing array of real estate holdings, as well as the prospect of working with an estranged aunt and a general lack of direction in how to manage an estate. That's a whole set of skills and knowledge that Alysa would have to work on with me and the other members of her team in the years to follow.

If you find yourself in a similar situation to Alysa's, you could try to sort it out alone, cowboy through it all, be the rugged Marlboro Man. That would be your first mistake. In Alysa's case, she appreciates her ability to make some sense out of the family's finances, but she's not exactly eager to stay up nights sorting it all out. If you really want to make something beautiful out of all this, given the amount of work facing you and the years of expertise you'll need at every turn, then start assembling your team of experts.

There are aspects of your life where you should be the star player. Namely your dreams, the things that are unique to your ideals, your imagination, and your aspirations. Please tell me that managing the unwanted, burdensome details of your inheritance is not your aspiration! Good. So take yourself off the field and leave the daily grind, the gridiron battles, the back-and-forth, to your designated team players. Out there on the field is a tough place to be; ask any old, arthritic sports star. You won't be turning your back. You can oversee from the sidelines; you can direct from the owner's box.

Back to your inheritance. Certain specialists are crucial for their specific areas of expertise and can provide critical advice on bigger issues that cross multiple fields. For instance, drafting a will involves an attorney and often a tax expert and sometimes a philanthropic advisor. In some cases, as many as six different specialists will weigh in on aspects of a key document like that. If you're ambitious, you may choose to take it upon yourself to coordinate, orchestrate, manage, and even motivate all the members of your team for such projects. But even in that role, inevitably, you could use a peer—an assistant coach.

When you take responsibility as owner of the team that manages your finances, that's a huge step forward—and eventually every inheritor should get there. For those just getting started, though, you probably said to the last paragraph: "*Peer? Assistant coach?!* I need someone to tell me what to do!" Fair enough. There are plenty of people out there you could turn to. Some are eager to help; others not so much. Some are competent; others not so much. The team analogy is helpful here. When starting a new team, who would you hire first? Loudmouth fans who will tell you how to run your team? A star player (without knowing the culture of your team as a whole yet)? The backup placekicker? I guess it was a loaded question: you need a coach.

Your Team Needs a Coach

Think about why coaches are so important in virtually every sport. This is someone with staying power to stick with the team as long as possible, through thick and thin. This is someone who is more a leader than a showoff, more a teacher than a star student. The coach is the one figure who can talk to the team owner as easily as the players in the locker room. A coach puts his or her heart into it, but does so with respect for the directives and vision of the team's owner. (The owner? That's you, by the way.)

Just as life coaches or executive coaches work one-on-one with individual clients, *wealth coaches* adapt their approach to whatever skills, advice, and support their client most needs at any given time. When you hear "wealth coach," you might have a vision of someone like a psychologist, firing out questions as you lounge on a couch in their office. But wealth coaches are typically more hands-on. I'm one, and I've been known to make personal calls on behalf of my clients, go on "field trips" to walk clients through new experiences, and sit in on meetings and conference calls for clients' wealth-related matters.

I've heard of a wealth coach who drove to a client's

house and installed her underground safe for her. He wasn't her handyman; he was the coach and advisor who, based on her situation, suggested she buy gold. He just happened to have the right power tools—and an attitude that said he should do whatever his clients needed. If you find a coach like that, you've got a keeper!

The skill set and knowledge that *any* wealth coach should be able to demonstrate includes: 1) a foundation in the financial details specific to inheritance, 2) a holistic approach to getting things done, and 3) most importantly, a true "coach" ethic. Above all else, this person is there to encourage you to achieve your potential, gauge your progress, and challenge you to develop the skills and abilities you'll need at each new step in your plan. Success is important, but arguably a coach's *more* important role is helping to navigate the darker or more confusing times. Nearly anyone can see a team through a familiar set of drills, but only a true coach can guide you against an unknown opponent. Honestly, that gameday scenario is more like the reality of inherited finances.

I have particular preferences for how to select a coach. As you read them, I think you will see where I'm coming from and create your own parallel preferences. If not, simply do exactly as I say and don't ask questions—just like my daughters did during their teenage years. *Yeah, right Mom, like whatever.*

Age and experience can be important factors for your

coach. Rookies don't walk into their first practice and take over a team. On the flipside, some veterans of sports (or, in this case, finance) get grizzled, hardened, and set in their ways. Remember, you're the leader. If they're going to pursue your ideals, then they must have compatible ideals or be flexible enough to see things your way.

Flexibility is important for more than just a personal compatibility with your team. The financial world is a constantly spinning globe. Surprises abound for even the savviest, most world-tested coaches. As mutual fund companies say in their fine print (please read double-time, in your best radio announcer voice), "Past performance does not guarantee future results."

You're looking not just for a fat résumé, but a coach who seems poised for whatever an uncertain future may throw at you—and the world. Think about a coach's job for a moment. Every winning team has a coach—and, *ahem*, every losing team has one, too. Winning is the easy part, whenever it actually happens. Or, as a colleague likes to say, "Rewards will take care of themselves; you have to focus on the risk side of the equation." Your job as leader and your other leaders' jobs are not merely to "win" but to make the most of your team, through wins, losses, and everything in-between.

Which Team Are They Playing For?

In the next section, we'll learn more about some other

players who should be on your wealth team, but first you need a tool for determining which side of the table each prospective consultant or advisor is on. Are they working in your best interests or theirs?

A helpful term here is *fiduciary*. It's not bandied about your local sports bar, but it's an important term in the world of the inheritor. A fiduciary is someone who is legally bound to represent another's best interests over their own. Here's the catch: While they may not be looking after their own interests, they aren't necessarily protecting yours. Some fiduciaries are bound to represent the best interests of an original wealth creator, even if that doesn't actually seem to be advancing the interests of the designated beneficiaries.

Some wealth coaches are fiduciaries. They sign an agreement (a.k.a. a fiduciary engagement letter and other variations) at the onset of your work with them, assuring you that they are not shilling for some parent company, hyping some product that gives them a kickback, or otherwise looking out for anyone's best interest but yours. Because you sign the fiduciary engagement letter with them, you can be assured that it's *you* they're working for. If I could wave my magic wand, I would make this a requirement for any inheritor to work with a wealth coach. I'd also make variations of this type of agreement common for the many other professionals on your team. While I search for my magic wand, you can at least take this little piece of advice to heart: Get as many signed fiduciary agreements as you can.

Your Team Needs Players

OK, perhaps this team thing is the longest running analogy of the book so far. It's like baseball, deep in extra innings. It's like triple overtime in hockey. It's like a curling match that goes till dawn. Hopefully it's helpful to think of your network of wealth advisors like a team; at least sports are a fun way to face adversity. You're not proud of the collarbone you broke slipping in the shower, but I bet you still show people your knee surgery scar from that spring-break skiing accident. Well, a good wealth management plan has both the crowd-pleasing acrials of skiing and those mundanely dangerous slippery bathroom surfaces. Get the right folks to handle each of those risks and you've got a team. Here are some of the positions you should consider filling on your team:

Wealth Coach – Whether you choose a wealth coach as your lead advisor or not, this should be a featured player on an inheritor's team. I could go on about wealth coaches, but I bet you get it.

Trustee – Defined simply, this is a designated representative who follows through on the terms of a trust. A *trust* is a legal entity, often funded with either real money or something of value—say ownership of a property or part of a company—that is for the benefit of the *beneficiary*. The beneficiary is whoever (or whatever) receives the benefits outlined in the trust. So, as just two of many possible examples, an individual beneficiary may receive regular payments, or a charitable organization might serve as a beneficiary by receiving a one-time donation. The terms of each trust, which the trustee has agreed to uphold, were set by the grantor. A trust's *grantor* is often the person who created the wealth in the first place.

Returning to the recent discussion of fiduciaries, trustees *are* fiduciaries. They must set aside their best interests—say, their own personal profit or that of their firm—to honor the intent of a trust. That *does* mean looking out for the health of the trust fund for the ultimate benefit of its beneficiaries, but note that the trustees are officially beholden to the trust itself and its grantor. That can mean they're responsible for safeguarding the trust's availability to *future* beneficiaries, not just you. And the specific wishes of the grantor may have included some restrictions on how much leeway you're allowed to have as beneficiary.

The tides are changing. Even "irrevocable trusts" and their caretakers can be held to higher standards.

As Jay Hughes explains in *Family Wealth*, the trustee-beneficiary relationship is often an arranged marriage. Quite frequently you don't choose your trustees—they are selected by your grantor. But as Hughes also points out, the tides are changing. Even "irrevocable trusts" and their supposedly unchallengeable caretakers can be questioned and held to higher standards today than ever before.

While Hughes has an earful for every trustee—he cautions them to "do no harm," always putting beneficiaries' needs ahead of their own—he doesn't let you off the hook either, Mr. or Ms. Inheritor. His list of "roles and responsibilities of beneficiaries," for instance, is actually longer than the same list for trustees. He wants you to do your homework, read all that legalese that you don't think you can understand, and build a base knowledge of the principles of wealth management to be an active, thoughtful participant in all your beneficiary/ trustee relationships. *Family Wealth* is a great place to start if you have a less-than-satisfactory arrangement with your trustee(s). It takes a refreshingly collaborative approach that I've found gives inheritors both the knowledge and the optimism to challenge the assumption that you don't have control of your wealth.

Whether you love them or hate them, trustees have a very important connection to you, the beneficiary, and your wealth. They are often in control of (though they typically don't *own*) resources that are likely to be yours one day. Simplifications like this belie the intricacies of the average trust. It's not as simple as "they have something of yours," but that's a step in the direction of understanding their role. Hughes is more succinct on this subject, although he sometimes hides his opinions coyly in footnotes. In one he admits: "I am not suggesting that trustees aren't part of the problem, because they are, and in the next chapter ... I'll discuss their roles and responsibilities." The irony is, of course, that Hughes is himself a trustee for many beneficiaries and is thus "part of the problem."

Though it makes this a long-winded explanation, I believe it's worth the time to understand what trustees are from their perspective as well as from your own. The best trustees (and I have no doubt Jay Hughes is among them) serve as genuine representatives and mentors to the clients and beneficiaries they represent. It can be a thankless job, but only when you and your trustee *both* fail to make it a positive collaboration toward a common goal. Hughes explains why he chooses to be part of the problem: "When people you deeply care about want to try to preserve their ... assets and values long into the future, the journey with them is too exciting to say no." You'd be lucky to land trustees with that level of passion for their work, but you'd be foolish not to give your trustees the opportunity to step up to the highest possible level of service and collaboration.[4]

---

[4] Jay Hughes, by the way, is actively retiring after many, many years of sterling service. I hope I haven't gotten you so excited about his abilities that you're ready to call and enlist him. Luckily he has written two books which have changed the very fabric of the trustee-beneficiary relationship. If you're

Attorney – When it comes to handling the demands of your legal counsel, there are a variety of specific experts, from estate tax and probate attorneys to litigators. There are also high-level attorneys and firms who can handle or oversee virtually any legality you face. Like many fields, law is a complex and constantly changing landscape—so the most valuable skill for you is the ability to ask good questions of the legal eagles on your team.

Easier said than done. You may not even know what types of legal advice you need, or you may be overlooking certain details of your situation that could really use the input of an attorney. Meanwhile, it's possible to hemorrhage immense amounts of money and your own valuable time on wild goose chases and unnecessary legal work. You'll want to select attorneys who, like the other members of your wealth team, can speak plainly, guiding you to the right questions, even when you don't know what to ask.

Even just knowing that you *can* select your attorneys is sometimes a revelation to inheritors. Certain aspects of your wealth may have designated trustees, executors, and family or corporate attorneys, but you may *always* solicit a second opinion or engage a specialist for certain questions.

---

looking to designate a trustee (or are having trouble wrangling the ones you're with), Hughes' books may prove an invaluable resource for both you and your trustees. Learn more in the "Further Resources" section at the back.

Like trustees, attorneys often appear in a seemingly unchallengeable role. You may not have selected them and you likely don't see easy recourse to replace them. (What are you gonna do, sue a lawyer?! It's a surprisingly common occurrence, despite the intimidation factor.) Here I adapt Jay Hughes' advice on trustees: If you're ready to sue yours, first look at yourself. Are you filling your end of the arrangement "with excellence"? Have you even read the documents in question—wills, trusts, etc.? Of course, you're only half the picture and there certainly are some bad eggs out there in the legal fields.

Hughes is quick to acknowledge trends that have beleaguered his beloved family profession recently (yes, he's an attorney as well as a trustee, the tortured soul). As he reports: "Most professional firms are no longer organized to solve their clients' problems. They are organized to sell products to their clients." This is not, in and of itself, bad—except that those products are being sold at inflated hourly rates that were meant for one-on-one, custom problem-solving services. When you consider an attorney as one of the captains of your team, you need that sort of a custom problem solver, not some franchise selling a blanket, trademarked solution.

Tax Accountant – Because your money has a history and, as I will browbeat in later chapters, a long future, there are options to explore for several generations looking both forward and backward. The list of tax categories is daunting: estate taxes, income taxes, property taxes, gift taxes, foreign taxes, and corporate taxes, plus dozens of other categories unique to certain types of businesses, trust funds, and wealth transfers. And that's to say nothing of the many complex processes required to calculate your liabilities within each tax category: deductions, depreciations, withholding, exclusions, and one itemized partridge in a pear tree.

As with attorneys, there are specialists in different fields of tax—a necessary fact in a field where annual tax code changes at the local, state, federal, and international levels could wallpaper the planet several times over. Also, like attorneys, there are generalists who are capable of sourcing and coordinating a team so that you remain in an informed, decision-making role without spending every night reading tax codes romantically by firelight.

Certified Public Accountant (CPA) – CPAs are an example of the generalists mentioned above who *typically* have a broad enough background in many tax areas to oversee most or all of a client's tax details. Though certification is a rigorous process, there are over 350,000 CPAs in the U.S., meaning there is a vast range of ability level and specialty. Of course this is an extremely oversimplified explanation for which I would probably get audited by the IRS and then flogged by any good CPA.

Certified Financial Planner (CFP®) – Typically focused on the future, CFP practitioners are, as their name suggests, *planners*. They don't merely handle retirement plans, life insurance, and investments—although these are commonly thought to be their specialties. The lines are not always strict in this field, but often these practitioners consult on big-picture financial questions and concerns. Don't be dazzled by certificates and plaques on your advisors' office walls—make sure you understand exactly what they do and where their expertise ends. I like to ask them point blank: "What is your core expertise?" If you ask them, "Will I need other experts?" and they say, "No," then run! Bolt as fast as you can! I would also ask them if they will agree to be a fiduciary for you; many will and many won't. If they won't, I say it's a big wide world; find one who will.

Executor, also known as a "personal representative" in some states – Even the most iron-clad wills can be misinterpreted, outdated by changing circumstances, or simply a ton of work to implement. In my opinion, the best executors are a certain type of person, someone uniquely capable of selflessly honoring the wishes of a will's creator, the deceased. When choosing your own will's executor, it's not necessarily the person closest to you or the person most like you—but rather an honorable, capable person who can understand the intent of your wishes and adapt and execute them in changing circumstances.

If, after you die, everything unfolds as you expected, then this person's job will be easy. But you want to select someone who can also react to changing tax codes, dissolution of philanthropic causes you had planned to support, or disagreements among the beneficiaries of your estate.

Planning for what happens when you're gone is not only uncomfortable, but it's an educated guess, a gamble, so name the person you think will be reliable in carrying out your wishes through thick and thin. It's actually important to consider practicalities such as whether this person has time to be your executor, or whether he or she is likely to survive you. Of course an individual executor can always hire others if he or she wants assistance. Institutional firms can fill the role of executor in many states, but you should treat them as if they were an individual signing a contract for services— any of their future representatives should uphold the same principles you initially establish.

Children's Custodian (a.k.a. Guardian) – One extremely important, and difficult, provision of any parent's will is determining who will care for minor children if the parent(s) dies. Like choosing an executor, this choice has severely personal ramifications. Depending on your children's age, you're choosing a surrogate parent. Not only do you need to consider what's best for the children, but you need to factor in your prospective custodian's own preferences and willingness. It's a difficult question, both to ask and to answer, since 1) you're addressing the specter of your own mortality and 2) you're making a plan B that is not what you had hoped for. Even after you've found an agreeable guardian, the terms of that arrangement—from details of legal custody and where the children may live to financial compensation for your guardian, provisions for cost of living, college funds, etc.—require careful consideration and (often) professional consulting.

Power of Attorney (POA) Designee – As long as you're considering morbid scenarios, there are numerous ways that you can lose your ability to direct your own wishes. Whether temporary or permanent, if you find yourself mentally, emotionally, or physically unable to direct the key decisions in your life, make sure you have chosen a reliable delegate to speak on your behalf. When you provide a power of attorney (or multiple POAs, such as different designees for your financial and medical decisions), you're assured that someone other than state authorities will speak for you when you can't. The terms of when and how the point of your incapacity will be determined are always critical components of any power of attorney document.

Insurance Advisor – There are several factors in your situation that mean you'll need more than the typical insurance agent. You might have properties and valuables in multiple states or countries, for instance; most insurance *agents* cannot offer coverage outside their state. The purpose of insurance is to protect you from catastrophe, that is, losses from which you cannot recover. But your specific definition of catastrophe is likely to be different than that of the general population. You can absorb a $5,000 deductible, for instance, but an ongoing medical problem could cost you millions (and it is unlikely that you have medical coverage through an employer). For many inheritors—especially when the majority of your net worth is made up of illiquid assets such as real estate—purchasing life insurance may provide you some estate tax benefits. Figuring out the best options may require collaboration between your tax and insurance experts. Hire an insurance *advisor* (who does not sell insurance products) to offer advice and coach you through implementing that advice.

Philanthropic Advisor – The world is full of great causes in dire need of support. It also includes a number of causes that don't match your values, your wishes, and your goals. It's not always easy to determine which is which—and then to decide among the best candidates. And this is to say nothing of the variables involved in determining *how* to support a worthy mission. In some cases, the right philanthropic move is to create something entirely new. All this amounts to what can be a full-time job (or even an entire organization's staff) to articulate your vision, build a plan, coordinate your resources, and implement your wishes.

Counselor – Some family issues transcend financial questions and require the services of a counselor, therapist, or psychiatrist to resolve. Emotional issues and mental illness can have very real, very painful effects on your financial realities and your ability to collaborate with (or even tolerate) your family members. When selecting among counselors, therapists, psychologists, life coaches, etc., make sure their philosophies and approaches resonate with your own values. Most important to any counseling engagement is your own openness to awkward and uncomfortable self-analysis—one that will depend on an underlying trust in your counselor's intent and approach.

Life Coach – Like a wealth coach, a life coach is someone who can guide and motivate you through life's bumpiest paths. Virtually anyone can coach—or coast through—a straight, paved road. The true test of a life coach is what he or she does for you when the twists and turns get hairy. Seek a coach with a common outlook on life,

and don't be afraid to ask the tough questions up front:
"How will you advise me when I'm at my wits' end?"
"How will you help me create the life I want to live?"

Personal Assistant – Unlike company secretaries or assistants
to whole departments (who must adapt to the multiple
personalities they serve), personal assistants must sync
up with your individual approach. Good assistants have
a holistic approach that emulates your style: They can be
a sounding board or a devil's advocate, but in the end,
they should be capable of making the same judgment
calls you would. Virtually anyone can *take* orders, but
the greatest value an assistant can bring you is the ability
to *make* orders that agree with you. That can save you
immense time prioritizing your to-do list, coping with
the unexpected, and simply getting things done.

**Miscellaneous: Driver, Cleaning Staff, Chef, Nanny,
Grounds-keeper, Handyman, Event Planner, Travel
Agent, Personal Trainer, Massage Therapist, Pool Guy,
Aquarium Gal, Flower Lady, Tutor, Wild Animal Wran-
gler** – Don't overlook or underestimate the value of a
reliable team to handle some or all of life's everyday
chores. It's not as simple as handing off every duty under
your roof, since some chores are actually fulfilling and
enjoyable. Indeed, everyday chores can be a necessary
grounding, calming, humbling exercise when all else in

life seems intense and overwhelming. Even the President of the United States chooses certain household chores to handle. Only you know (or can discover) which tasks you love and which are drudgery. Imagine you are the multimillion-dollar salaried CEO of a public company whose time is immensely valuable to your stakeholders. That would dictate two key priorities: 1) Minimize time spent on unfulfilling tasks that can be delegated, and 2) hang on to the projects that enrich your life and make you better balanced to deal with everything else on your plate. We'll address this further in Chapter 6, but for now you can rest assured that you won't have to clean up after your son's pet boa constrictor for much longer.

Manage Your Managers

That list of team players to consider is a long one, to be sure, and there are numerous other professionals you can choose for a high-level role in your wealth management plan. From financial advisors to life coaches, your own strengths and interests, as well as the details of your portfolio, will be the best guides for whom to consult. If the hard finances of your situation are the most baffling or frustrating of all the challenges you face, you may want an investment advisor or wealth management analyst to be your primary consultant. If interpersonal issues or your own soul searching feel like the first order of business, then a life coach or family counselor may be your mentor of choice.

Your team may include just a couple of the above players or it may place several people in each position. In the end (and at points of confusion along the way), I like to come back to that sports team analogy that I haven't quite beaten dead yet: You've got a game to play. When overwhelmed by minutia, don't lose sight of your ultimate goals. If in doubt, there's no reason you can't call a huddle-up, a gathering of your top advisors, and solicit the group's feedback on what's next and where you're headed.

> *A leader must have the courage to act*
> *and to act against an expert's advice.*
> JAMES CALLAGHAN,
> FORMER UK PRIME MINISTER

As team leader, just because you asked the question, you certainly don't have to accept the answers. Be involved, demand plain talk and open communication, and don't settle for anything less than your team's very best. How's that for a halftime pep talk?

One simple benefit of your situation as an inheritor is that you have financial resources at your disposal. You can afford good players, reliable advisors, and a top-notch coach. Bring them all together and sometimes you don't even have to ask all the intelligent questions. But don't get lazy. No matter who you are, you've got brains enough to comprehend the basic principles of every aspect of your wealth plan. Take your role as leader seriously and those you lead will take you seriously, too. Part of that authority comes from your willingness to learn the fundamentals of wealth conservation.

You are willing, aren't you?

CHAPTER FIVE

Philosophies and Strategies of Wealth Conservation

Beware the investment activity that produces applause;
the great moves are usually greeted by yawns.
WARREN BUFFETT TO HIS SHAREHOLDERS, 2008

Trusts, Risks, and the Concept of Wealth Conservation

Inheritors often have at least part of their wealth held in a trust. While there are many types, trust funds are typically structured to be a *caretaker of assets for a beneficiary.* The term "trust" derived from the Roman concept of use, meaning, in essence, that someone else may *use* something of yours for a while without actually owning it. This all began in warlike times when a lord went off to battle and left his estate in the hands of a trusted delegate, often a member of the clergy.

The concept, then and now, is that after a predetermined amount of time, the assets are delivered back with at least their original value. It's sort of like loaning out your golf clubs and asking that they be returned without the driver being bent in half or the sand wedge left behind in a bunker. A consideration with financial assets is that inflation changes the value of money. So a million dollars put in trust will ultimately be worth less over time, unless it has been invested and grown in pace with the cost of living. With money the goal is to maintain purchasing power, so conservation requires growth.

There are, of course, degrees of risk in every portfolio management plan. It's hard not to think of portfolio theories as cleverly disguised styles of gambling. They are. Higher risk investments have the potential for more growth and, conversely, more risk of dropping in value.

Ah, "risk." It's sad but true—risk cannot be avoided. Maybe that's just as well: What kind of life would you have if you never took risks? In cards, risk is a complex but calculable set of odds. There is a finite number of cards, there is a set of strict rules for whatever game you're playing, and there is the potential (for really brainy and methodical types, like the MIT crew that soaked a Las Vegas casino) to actually manage the game and all but guarantee big profits.

The real world you inhabit is no card game. The number

of factors that can, and do, affect the value of your estate through the years is astronomical. The layers of complexity that impact how different factors affect each other—and the dynamics of change and surprise—mean that there are no laws, no strict rules in *this* game. So estate planning becomes a fascinating mix of theories, mathematical projections that are no more than tools—and often dubious ones at that—along with gut-level instincts. Study the past, analyze the present, and predict the future. Simple, right? Making sense of the past and present is tough enough, but *predicting the future?*

With all those caveats duly noted, there really are guiding principles and respected theories in this business. It's not entirely a crapshoot. And at the higher levels of inheritance— what I generally view as fortunes valued at $25 million or more—the available resources are likely to be sufficient to last a lifetime if managed prudently and not spent to excess. Put another way, chances are that if you choose not to work (for pay) another day in your life, your assets should sustain a more than reasonable lifestyle. I think that's where it gets interesting, which is why I've chosen to work primarily with inheritors at this level. Other wealth coaches have different specialties, and even the others in my office specialize in certain other financial circumstances, but I'm funny that way: I like working with people who face these particular challenges and this kind of potential.

Of course it's an arbitrary number, but for some with

less than a $25 million net worth, though they are likely to afford *anything* they want, they might not be able to afford *everything* they want. It all depends on their levels of "satiation spending" (addressed in the next chapter; no jumping ahead). Either way, it starts with that little phrase I sneaked into the last paragraph: "if managed prudently and not spent to excess." When talking with financial people, I would describe this as a "low-volatility portfolio." With the rest of the world, I would call this "wealth conservation."

It's important to understand that I'm a little unusual in my focus on *conservation* for inheritors. I suspect it's the conflict of interest (dare I say greed?) of commission-based investment advisors that creates unnecessary risk in the management of such portfolios. I'm not suggesting inheritors hoard their first $25 million under their mattress; that would be risky indeed! But I really think it's foolish to put *all* of a fortune this size into play at the most uncertain levels of this game.

Many investment advisors—or wealth managers—charge a percentage of assets under management, so there's an incentive for the assets to grow. The more they grow, the more the advisors make. I recommend finding an advisor who charges a flat fee, based on the complexity of your situation. That way there's less conflict of interest if you, say, consider paying off your mortgage or want to give money to charity (both of which would put fewer funds under management). In my mind, the goal for inheritors at this level isn't necessarily accumulating wealth but *utilizing* your wealth in ways that help you seize your potential and enrich your life.

Now there's a detail I'm glossing over here. It's extremely rare that an inheritor's assets are all in one bundle, with a crystal clear value and total liquidity like a briefcase full of cash. Wealth is more typically tied up in trust funds, equity ownership of companies, properties, and other non-liquid forms. You probably don't have 100 percent freedom to determine the investment strategy for all your money, but you *do* have a say, no matter how your advisors, trustees, or executors try to intimidate you. When you have confidence in your convictions, you can't be bullied; and so the job of your best advisors or wealth coach should be to support your education in the relevant details of wealth conservation. When they can build your knowledge and your confidence, you can bet they are helping you build your potential.

"Modern" Theories Get an Education from the School of Hard Knocks

To begin to understand what your options might be, I recommend an expedited education in the history and so-called basics of investing:

Modern Portfolio Theory – Despite calling itself "modern," MPT is a set of ideas now generally considered the "old school" of investing. It includes principles such as **diversification**, or the distribution of eggs into many baskets. The theory is that by having assets in many distinct investments, your risk is spread out, and any single collapse will not devastate your portfolio. What has been all too often overlooked is that this is still a gamble, as the markets demonstrated in the second half of 2008. In that debacle, we saw that a stock market crash and its aftermath can still wreak havoc on a well-diversified portfolio.

Asset Allocation – There is mathematical backing for the concept of diversification that goes much deeper than counting eggs and baskets. Similarly, there are systems of evaluating individual investment options to predict whether their combination of likely risks and rewards actually improves the overall risk/reward balance of your portfolio. The logic is that some investments are risky in different ways than others; so when you stack them all up, you improve your odds of weathering the various storms that affect finances. You might think of it as putting each of your three pigs in a different type of house, on the theory that a big bad wolf is unlikely to have the tenacity (or lung power) to huff and puff and blow down all three types of construction.

If you really want to get into it, asset allocation created techniques for categorizing different classes of investments—say, stocks, bonds, real estate, gold bars, and money in Mason jars. In theory, it simplified the process of evaluating the risk/reward components of each asset in your estate, so that you could draw conclusions more quickly about what to keep and what to change.

Whoa there. There were some key phrases in that explanation upon which you should expend some critical thought: *predict, logic, improve your odds, in theory.* Every investment advisor relies on tools, simplifications, theories, and educated guesses to guide their actions. But beware whenever you're offered a prediction, a projection, a calculation, or a model that doesn't include a disclaimer. 2008 saw the debunking of modern, widely accepted theories of investment here in America and all over the world. 2008–2009 also saw criminals like Bernie Madoff and Robert Allen Stanford working scams that have been around for hundreds of years and shockingly still attract suckers and the uneducated. Even when there were disclaimers on those disasters, they were too easily dismissed or glossed over. If an investment scheme doesn't disclose some risk—or if it's disclosed and downplayed, or if it sounds too good to be true—it's probably not for you.

Inheritors' circumstances are unconventional, so conventional approaches to finance and investing generally aren't a good match for you. In my field, as a CFP® practitioner, most of our training and education is focused on wealth *accumulation*, not conservation. That's not a bad thing, since most of the population *is* concerned about having enough wealth to support themselves throughout their lives. But for the inheritor who has enough to support his or her lifestyle for a lifetime, it's time to set aside that all-American drive to accumulate more, focusing instead on protecting what you have.

Volatility Is Not Your Friend:
Riding out a Lifetime of Ups and Downs

It's easy to poke holes in any theory of investing simply because there really are no hard and fast laws in this business. But at some point you've got to have a plan for your money. I don't pretend to be a consummate investment expert myself, but—as I'm coaching you to do—I surround myself with experts I trust. I trust them because they look me in the eyes, explain their approach, and, frankly, don't go the way most other investment managers do. I like black sheep.

Coincidentally, I find many of my clients—the types of inheritors who are interested in seizing the potential of their wealth—are also the black sheep of their families. I mean the good kind of black sheep, the ones who go the other way when the flock seems headed for danger. Investing for many generations in the future is definitely not the way the Wall Street flock is running.

As Steve Henningsen, my business partner and the firm's primary investment expert, explains, "It's not so much about how much you make when the market's up as how little you lose when the market's down." His is not the most razzle-dazzle of sales pitches, *and I like that.* The arithmetic here is fairly simple and, sadly, the market gave us an example of its downside in 2008–2009. To test out the math, here's a hypothetical example, one that's a little too close to recent reality for many disheartened stock market players.

- You have an original investment portfolio balance of $100 million.
- Assume your investments are in line with the market as a whole (say the S&P 500).
- Say you lost **50 percent** of your portfolio value in 2008, like many investors really did.
- Now say the market rallies **40 percent** in two and a half months as it did mid-2009.
- 40 percent *of your remaining $50 million* is $20 million, bringing your portfolio to $70 million.
- So you're still down $30 million—or 30 percent of what you started with.

How did 100 minus 50 plus 40 add up to 70? It's tempting—but wrong—to oversimplify the numbers. You can't add and subtract percentages like dollars, but Wall Street and the whole finance industry tend to report things in these relative terms.

The operative principle here is *negative compounding*. You may have heard the reverse principle, "the miracle of compound interest." *That* concept is the upside of the logarithmic curve: When your money is steadily growing in value, you're making money on an ever larger pool of money, which means it snowballs—*hypothetically*. Of course, the world doesn't actually work like that. As one 17th-century apple enthusiast named Isaac Newton pointed out, what goes up must come down. And in the convoluted cycles-within-cycles merry-go-round that is the investment world, there are always going to be plenty of ups and downs.

When you look at the downs, the same compounding principle works, but in the other way. When you're losing value, you need a higher percentage gain to get you back to where you were. Lose 50 percent of your value, it's going to take 100 percent *of your new value* in gains just to get back to where you started. For those not numerically inclined, I hope the lesson here is clear: It's better not to lose money. Anyone not with me on that?

Stocks, mutual funds, virtually all things for sale are generally sold based on their recent performance—their notable gains. Human nature, or at least the new human nature in the age of marketing, tends to be sucked in by impressive statistics, not bothering with getting to the bottom of less than impressive numbers.

How sexy, for instance, does an eight percent average annual return sound? It doesn't hold a candle to TV ads for yesterday's hottest new investment firm, but here's another example of misleading math. There are two ways—two *approved* ways—to calculate an eight percent average simple return on an investment. One includes *no volatility*; your investment actually gains by that amount every year. And given the "miracle" of compound interest (really just simple arithmetic), the upward curve picks up speed as you continue making money not only on your original balance, but also on your annual investment gains.

The other way to calculate an eight percent average simple annual return is *with volatility*. This technique takes an average from several years of varying performance, which is a common practice (but easily abused, as you'll see in the chart below). A portfolio that gains 41 percent every other year, for instance, while losing just 25 percent in the interim years, technically averages an eight percent positive annual return. How do two such varied results claim the same "average return"? Quite simply, the volatility example is calculated from the original balance, while the low-volatility eight percent is constantly recalculated on the fly. Observe:

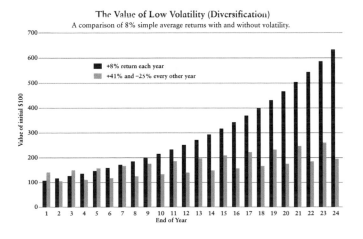

The Value of Low Volatility (Diversification)
A comparison of 8% simple average returns with and without volatility.

Note that in years one, three, and five, the volatile (gray) investment actually provides a higher portfolio value. That's a crucial time frame for the typical investor, lured by the marketing glamour of a portfolio that has the excitement of these big annual returns every other year and seems to be outperforming the low-volatility portfolio a full five years into the study. But, in this hypothetical example, year five is the last one where volatility "pays," and in fact two of those first five years it underperformed the low-volatility approach.

Here I go talking about a chart when a real human being is reading my book and saying, Myra—I'm not a chart. Hello, yes, I'm sorry. Don't underestimate how counterintuitive this "minimizing volatility," and "losing less" approach is when just about everything sold or marketed to you out there promises "more," "better," or "faster." By contrast, consider a scene from the Dudley Moore film (oh dear, I'm dating myself) *Crazy People*. Moore's character becomes disillusioned with his ad agency job and enlists the help of an insane asylum to help him come up with slogans such as this one for United Airlines: "Most of our passengers get there alive."

Go ahead, laugh. And please watch it—it really is a funny movie. Now think about it again. While everyone knows planes can and do crash, people really don't want to think about it—or plan for it happening to themselves or their loved ones. But if we take crashes as a given, wouldn't it actually be a good thing if an airline could say it has fewer crashes than the others? Same goes for your investment philosophy. From the perspective of lifelong wealth conservation, any short-term "all roses, no thorns" approach starts to sound like a plane that never needs a mechanic—now *that's* crazy, people.

From what I know of card-counting schemes (like the real-life MIT caper that was somewhat fictionalized in the book *Bringing Down the House* and heavily Hollywoodized in the film *21*) successful gambling—like successful investing—is about negotiating the

Someone prepared to manage funds for a lifetime—your lifetime—better not dismiss these as anomalies. Downturns are a long-term reality of every financial market.

risks, rather than chasing the long-shot big gains. There is calculated risk, and there are mitigated downturns. When the odds turn and the number of favorable cards is declining, it's time to pick another table that your partner has been tracking—one that has a higher likelihood to be heading into a favorable cycle.

There's a key: the *partner*. The MIT group's card caper was based on teamwork. There was a network of trained experts in that casino, carefully studying, analyzing, and tracking the trends at multiple promising tables. Now journey with me back from semi-fictionalized casino scams to your life. You're in an elite tier of wealth where you can—

and should—enlist a team to, in a sense, do the same thing. Couldn't you use a team that will determine all the various options and alert you to their trends and prospects, while keeping an eye on the future?

As convoluted as all of this can sound, it really boils down to one simple piece of advice: ask prospective investment advisors how they fared when the market tanked. Think of the collapse of tech stocks in 2000. Think of the collapse of just about everything in the market in 2008. Someone prepared to manage funds for a lifetime—*your* lifetime—better not dismiss these as anomalies. Downturns are a long-term reality of any, and every, financial market.

Planning for More than Three Generations

I'm seeking compatriots in the battle to erase yet another inheritance myth, that old phrase "shirtsleeves to shirtsleeves in three generations." That's the old curse—commonly believed in many societies worldwide—that a family's money is unlikely to survive beyond its third generation. Jay Hughes is one of my compatriots; he has what I consider a very helpful outlook on what it takes, starting with long-term thinking. Hughes cites a certain personal affection—one that transcends pure botanical allure—for the copper beech tree. As he explains, this particular tree is emblematic of a commitment to planning for more than today, more than one lifetime, and even more than 100 years:

Think of the courage it takes to plant a tree that takes
150 years to mature ... someone must invest love and
patience to nurture it. Think of the hurricanes, ice and
snow, pests, and fire that may consume the tree while
it is too young to withstand those hazards. It needs
help to survive those threats ... As it matures, it has to
contend with humans who want to cut it down for its
wood, and with governments that want to put a road or
a new housing development where it stands. The issues
the growing tree faces parallel those in the unfolding
life of a family.[5]

With stock tickers that change by the minute, daily
market reports, and property values fluctuating more than
annually, it shouldn't be surprising that the world tends to
take a very short-term view on finance. Where's the nightly
news story on the progress of a hundred-year investment
plan? It would be like reading second-by-second updates
on the progress of a snail crossing your lawn toward your
gardenias.

Revisiting for a moment the discussion on risk, there
is a tendency to call certain very conservative investments,
like government bonds, "zero risk." When working with
inheritors who want to defy the shirtsleeves myth, I ask
you to adopt a broad view of time, one that sees more than

---

[5] While this amazing tree is Hughes' favorite metaphor and makes an appearance
in both of his books, this particular quote is from *Family Wealth*, p. 13.

three generations into the future. That can be 100 years or more, the life of a copper beech tree and beyond. Looking that far ahead, I consider that there is no such thing as zero risk. Think about it: Governments have failed in less time, companies rarely survive a century, and even banks often vanish before your grandchildren are born (the understatement of the decade). So there's an element of the unknown you need to consider when managing your inheritance: your wealth could, and should, still be around in a time of flying cars and robot butlers.

Have you started saving for your great-grandchildren's cyborg immune system upgrade fund? Have you factored in depreciation on your family's Martian vacation home? I know all this sounds silly, but what would your great-great-grandparents have said in 1904 about your plans to invest in a company called Google in 2004? "Can you tell me what they *do* again, sweetie?"

The bottom line is that this kind of long-term perspective requires more than just financial modeling and precise asset allocation. You've actually got to look at the big picture of what you're creating and which direction

> *Core values don't change quickly. Sharing yours with future generations: Now that's a model for long-term wealth conservation.*

you hope it will go. I believe that we have a slim chance of guaranteeing a certain number of dollars or acres any time in the future. As just two examples of financial wealth, the value of money and of land—meaning their relative importance in our lives—just changes too much from generation to generation. What doesn't change as quickly are our core values. Identify yours, then build an infrastructure to share them with future generations, and then you'll have a model for long-term wealth conservation.

There's no reason human values can't drive wealth management more than financial concerns. As markets rise and fall, people still seem to find meaning and direction in their lives. Put your money in service to your value system, and you'll find it's piggybacking on something far more predictable than the stock market.

Stewardship and Conservation over Accumulation or Hoarding

As you can tell, I'm fond of the term *conservation* applied to wealth. It's especially powerful if you put it in the context of wildlife or nature conservation. In those cases, we're not talking about some behind-glass museum collection (that's what we do with the extinct species, or at least dead specimens), but rather the protecting and nurturing of living, breathing organisms and ecosystems. *Stewardship* has different, but complementary, connotations: visions of steering a ship, being responsible for guiding something much larger than just one person. In both cases, there is an inherent potential waiting to be seized. Living organisms and ecosystems are complex, evolving things; a ship is a huge convergence of engineering, crewmember collaboration, and a wise captain. Both stewardship and conservation imply a greater responsibility than just for your own skin. The job is not an easy one, but the rewards are staggering.

The alternate views of accumulation and hoarding, though common and widely accepted, are fundamentally archaic. I think of old tales of dragons lurking on piles of gold, long-bearded kings with treasures locked in castles, and all the accompanying bloodshed as others try to get their hands on the hoard. Hoarding, from an ecological stand-point, is the equivalent of plastic in a landfill that doesn't turn back to soil. We can learn from the natural world: It is not a warehouse, it is a turnstile, a constant exchange of resources. The eloquent environmentalist Dana Meadows made the point:

The planet does not get bigger, it gets better. Its creatures learn, mature, diversify, evolve, create amazing beauty and novelty and complexity, but live within absolute limits.[6]

Without recognition of these natural limits, we're guilty of unrealistic goals of consumption and accumulation. When recognizing limits, we then make the most of what we have and what is here for all of us—and we learn what they

---

[6] From Meadows' "The Laws of the Earth and the Laws of Economics" (full reference at end of book)

tried to teach us in kindergarten: *share*. Sharing is a form of diversification; it spreads your assets (both financial and intellectual) among other competent caretakers. In the long term view, the future will be in more hands than just your own, so begin the process with a spirit of stewardship and conservation during your lifetime.

Anticipating Change and Coping with the Unexpected

By the time you have adopted a long-term view of your finances, grasped your connection to the story of your wealth, and developed a sound investment philosophy of stewardship and conservation, you should be well prepared to handle many changes ahead. But what fun would that be? Thank fully for lovers of adventure, the world has a special way of surprising even the most doggedly prepared. The unexpected is not always a financial setback. Haphazard genetics can give a child Down Syndrome. The Grim Reaper doesn't always call ahead for an invitation. Wacky life dreams can intrude on the most sensible of lifestyles. Good, bad, and ugly turns of events can suddenly redirect your time, your visions, and your finances.

If you get in touch with your heart and gut (the organs I associate with your core values) and the substance of your soul, you're tuning into a compass that is more likely to guide you through uncertainties than an eye toward some future financial goal. An old parable from the East goes something like this:

A young man once sought out a well-known instructor of martial arts. He said, "I would like to become the greatest martial artist in all the land. How long must I study?"

The instructor told him, "Ten years, at least."

The young man frowned, saying, "That is a long time. What if I studied twice as hard as the other students? How long would that take?"

"Twenty years."

Quite frustrated now, the young man asked, "Why, if I work harder than the other students, do you tell me it will take twice as long?"

"It is simple," said the instructor, "with one eye fixed upon your destination, there is only one eye left with which to find the way."[7]

Sort of recalls the tortoise and the hare, right? The point is that there aren't any shortcuts. You can, in fact, slow down your progress in life if you become fixated on a finish line. The alternative? Listen to your heart and your gut and let their voices weigh in on your direction and your plan.

If your heart and gut speak like mine, though, you may need some help translating. For instance, how do you follow your heart on investment decisions that never made any sense to you in the first place? How do you trust your

---

[7] Paraphrased from Charles Ralph Heck's *Instructing the Martial Arts* (1988), p. 66

gut when you don't even understand the terminology in the questions you're asked? That's where I counsel inheritors to employ experts who can break down the walls of jargon that surround their respective fields. When an advisor can explain a decision you're facing in simple terms—such as listing the pros and cons of your options—then you can use both head and heart/gut to make your decision.

Your core values may well be the only things you can count on down the twists and turns of life into an uncertain future. When the flying cars and robot butlers arrive, only your heart will tell you which scenic backroads to fly for the afternoon and only your gut will know which flavor-pellets to order for lunch.

Now *getting in touch* with the substance of your soul, your core values, the desires of your heart, and the inclinations of your gut: that's not something easily dismissed. But it's an ongoing quest you should pursue your whole life and an exploration I encourage you to undertake as soon as possible. How about just as soon as we wrap up this book?

Lucky You: The Special Challenges Most Inheritors Face

Core values and highfalutin ideals aside, there are some very real, very specific financial decisions facing most inheritors. I saved them for the end of the chapter, hoping you would at least read this far. And honestly I think the highfalutin stuff comes first. If you aren't in touch with the bigger picture and your deeper values, you aren't prepared to lead your wealth team to the right solutions to these types of common situations.

- Are you paying too much tax on certain investment returns?
- Are your investments positioned to minimize volatility?
- Can you consolidate and simplify funds to save time and accounting costs?
- Is your portfolio diversified among managers?
- Do the terms of your trust nullify your prenuptial agreement?
- Are you carrying insurance on a painting you haven't owned for years?
- Have you taken full advantage of the annual gift exclusion?
- Did you file a gift-tax return for the stock you gave to your niece?
- Is your ILIT or CRT[8] set up and administered correctly?

---

[8] OK, guilty: I couldn't resist throwing a few acronyms in the list just for fun. Decoder key: If set up properly, an ILIT (Irrevocable Life Insurance Trust) can own a policy on your life without the proceeds from the policy being included in your taxable estate. CRTs, or Charitable Remainder Trusts, typically provide some distributions within an inheritor's lifetime, but ultimately benefit a charity (which can create tax benefits for the creator). These are just a sampling of the alphabet soup of options awaiting inheritors. You could study up and memorize them all—or you could find advisors who speak plainly to you about these options. Guess which one I recommend.

Perhaps some specific examples would help. In the next chapter we'll explore a few case studies to give you an idea of the specific decisions, options, challenges, and opportunities that are likely awaiting you.

CHAPTER SIX

Your Plan, Your Life, Your Legacy

We don't do forecasts, we only make guesses about the future based on irrational varying degrees of confidence.
JACK CROOKS, INVESTMENT MANAGER

Your Financial Snapshot

OK, let's get into the nuts and bolts of wealth. So how much do you have? What's the number? How much are you worth (not from your mother's perspective, but from the view of your accountant and banker)? Answer those questions quickly and with confidence, and I'll suspect you're a practiced liar. Setting aside for now the non-monetary aspects of wealth, the intellectual capital, the underlying values, the momentum it carries—there are far more than just bank balances and portfolio values to consider here. Take Alysa's original financial snapshot, for instance:

NOTE 1

Though collecting data for your snapshot may seem tedious, it just gets easier after the first time. A good wealth coach or advisor can help you establish a filing system, teach you which paperwork to shred (and when), set up electronic statements, and more.

NOTE 3

As the bigger picture came together, we were able to combine similar details, such as Yia Yia's 15 wholly-owned properties versus her two partial ownerships, to reduce clutter and aid in analysis.

♀ ALYSA'S FINANCIAL SNAPSHOT

INITIAL VERSION

List of Investment Assets

ASSETS

Taxable Investments
Schwab Acct.
North Bessemer Trust
Total Taxable Investments

Tax-Deferred Investments
Schwab Roth Account
Schwab IRA Account
Smith Johnson IRA
Total Retirement Investments
Total Investments

Other Assets (est. net of liabilities)
Private Investment
Boulder Condo
1/2 Miami Townhouse (equity)
1/2 Breckenridge Condo
Miami Residence
North Carolina Residence
Breckenridge Office Building
Breckenridge, Empty Lot
48th Street Apartments, Miami
Terrace Apartments, Miami
Dallas Strip Mall
Coral Gables Apartments (equity)
Miami Villas
Edgewater Land
Hernando Commercial Property, Phoenix
Georgia Lots
Wyoming Ranch
Vermont Retreat Center/Spa

Total Other Assets

TOTAL NET WORTH

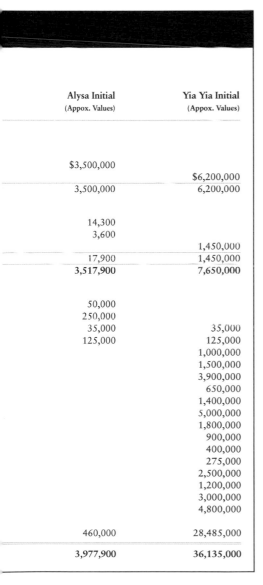

Alysa Initial (Appox. Values)	Yia Yia Initial (Appox. Values)
$3,500,000	
	$6,200,000
3,500,000	6,200,000
14,300	
3,600	
	1,450,000
17,900	1,450,000
3,517,900	7,650,000
50,000	
250,000	
35,000	35,000
125,000	125,000
	1,000,000
	1,500,000
	3,900,000
	650,000
	1,400,000
	5,000,000
	1,800,000
	900,000
	400,000
	275,000
	2,500,000
	1,200,000
	3,000,000
	4,800,000
460,000	28,485,000
3,977,900	36,135,000

NOTE 2

Alysa's grandmother wanted to begin sharing her wealth with Alysa without excessive tax consequences. By creating a balance sheet of assets and liabilities, we helped identify her best options.

NOTE 4

Once this initial snapshot was completed, all future updates could be easily compared to the original, allowing for powerful investment tracking, identification of areas where the estate is overly exposed to risk, detailed projections, and specific plans for the future.

As you assemble your financial snapshot, you will likely notice that certain facets change, sometimes significantly, as often as daily and weekly. Don't sweat absolute accuracy down to hours and minutes. The point is to get a fairly succinct understanding of all that you have at this point in time so you can plan, track, and modify your strategy for the future. You'll need this snapshot of where you stand now because certain assets do change significantly over time, and entirely new elements can come to light seemingly out of nowhere.

New developments—whether expected or unexpected, good, bad, or confusing—can change your financial standing. Additional inheritances, market booms and busts, corporate restructurings ... you could drive yourself crazy trying to anticipate every future development. Please don't. Simply note the expected and potential future developments: maturity or termination dates on trust funds, years left on your CRT's income, investment gains, and the like. Don't be afraid to ask all the questions that occur to you, and further, ask the experts if there are *other* questions you should be asking.

Figuring out the right questions to ask is easier said than done. Most fortunes have layers of diversification, making them complex to sort out. From the standpoint of investment philosophy, that's generally good, but it tends to make it a pain to determine your starting point. Real estate with shifting market values, trust funds that mature gradually over time, property you co-own with others, protected assets that are protected either *for* you or *from* you ... determining what you have can be an arduous process.

Do not be discouraged at the amount of research, calls, and paperwork that may be involved in determining your starting point. Feel free to take it in baby steps: Give it 30 minutes a day, for instance, or two entries a day, until it's done. Without an initial benchmark that shows what you have at your disposal now (and what is set aside and protected for you later), any planning you do for your future is guesswork. We're talking about your health and happiness throughout your lifetime: comfort in your later years, inheritance you will leave for others, college funds. Do you want to leave all that to guesses?

Some advisors will turn you loose to gather all the info with nothing more than a checklist and a "good luck." Others will offer to do the research for you. Personally, I recommend you outsource as much of the work as possible to trusted advisors for efficiency and accuracy. Inevitably some details may be easier for you to gather, like bank statements you may have filed. But poring over the fine print of trust documents, wills, property deeds, and other sorts of paperwork—anything that makes your eyes feel like hayfever season—there are often just too many details. Some of these details are important enough to impact the value of your assets and debts—and others can eat up hours, days, and weeks of your life without any benefit. Those are the details that are often most efficiently handled by pros.

That said, I will inevitably eat my own words before this book is through. I will challenge you—and, frankly, I encourage *any* beneficiary of any significant trust—to read and understand your trust documents, your will, tax returns, balance sheets, and much more. Though I do want you to build a strong team and delegate much of the work ahead, you don't get to simply check out after that. I have bigger plans for you!

Once your snapshot is assembled, it's due for some high-level analysis. Some "assets," for instance, can feel more like liabilities. I see this often with inherited property: It's not unusual for inheritors to own, say, 1/12th of a ranch or house that requires cash contributions to pay for maintenance and upgrades. When such a "gift" creates negative cash flow for the recipient, it's perfectly understandable to feel frustrated or even swindled.

In analyzing Alysa's snapshot, the to-do list for her wealth management team started with such items as:

❦ **ALYSA**
Some of the Tasks Facing Her Team
1. Create a family limited partnership combining some of Yia Yia's estate with selected assets belonging to Alysa. Among other benefits, this provided increased legal liability protection for their assets.
2. Make Alysa a salaried general partner for the partnership. This gave Alysa the opportunity to earn an

income: providing both a source of self-worth for her
as well as a sensible way to transfer Alysa's intended
share of Yia Yia's estate without incurring gift or
generation-skipping taxes.

3. Transfer all out-of-state properties into the partnership.
This eliminated the need to file probate in eight separate
states, saving significantly on attorney costs and red
tape that would have been involved otherwise.

Of course each inheritor's situation will be different.
From the seemingly simple (never believe it!) to the impossibly complex (nothing's impossible, right?), I would place
Alysa's situation somewhere in the middle. She's got her work
cut out for her, but the details seem manageable. Taking the
time to identify the decisions for which clocks are ticking
and the places where your wealth is needlessly at risk are
crucial steps in unburdening your wealth. And if hearing
about ticking clocks and "crucial steps" brings on labored
breathing, don't forget my "don't panic" clause: You can
afford to take the time to make good decisions.

Once your snapshot's done, or at least well underway,
it's time to take a more general look at your needs throughout your life.

Satiation Spending and Defining Your Nut

You've been allocated one lifetime; that's it. Regardless
of the source of your wealth, regardless of whether you're

planning a legacy that will survive you, you have until the day you die to achieve your dreams. True, you can create legacies that will carry your visions beyond your grave, but you've got to envision those plans and set them in motion while you're still here. So an important step in wealth planning is to assure you'll have enough to satisfy your needs and desires throughout your life expectancy. That's called securing your "nut" (finally, a financial term from the squirrels rather than a Scrabble® triple-word-score Hall of Famer).

Start by defining and articulating how you want to spend your money throughout your life: I call this "satiation spending." This will be much more than your Christmas list for Santa—a good wealth coach can guide you through the process. Together you'll take what you have and what you plan to spend, mapping that over a realistic projection of your lifespan. You'll extrapolate a return on your investment, an inflation rate, a life expectancy, and *voila!* That's how you'll determine if you have enough assets to meet all your needs and wants.

The nut is the amount that supports your satiation spending beyond your expected lifespan. It requires consideration of investment returns, changing personal circumstances, market fluctuations, and on and on. Like so much in this process, it's an arbitrary calculation, though not *random:* inherently flawed but helpful nonetheless. The flaw is that nobody can see the future. For instance, in 2004 you never saw a nut calculation that anticipated the 50 percent market slide in

2008-2009, but a good calculation will specifically address and provide reasonable flexibility to accommodate such surprises. Where nut calculations are helpful is taking your financial snapshot—your sense of where you stand now—and telling you whether you're likely to have enough.

The chart below illustrates Mary's simplified nut calculation. Like Alysa, her financial snapshot had established her net worth. Her exposure analysis refined her available assets and the costs of maintaining her estate. With the nut calculation, we constructed her likely wealth circumstances throughout her lifetime.

❋ **MARY**

Living Like a Pauper While Her Fortune Awaits

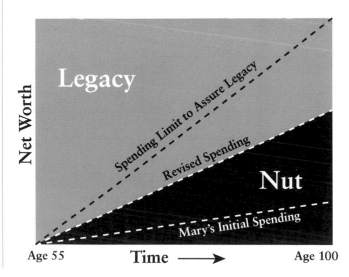

Mary's initial spending habits were frugal to say the least. That's not necessarily a bad thing, except that coaching revealed she was pinching her pennies solely out of shame. After so many years of hiding her wealth from others, she'd managed to hide it from herself as well, living as if she had to scrimp to make it through her lifetime. Nothing could have been further from the truth.

All those years, she had neglected passions that were well within her means. Her nut calculation very quickly confirmed that she was due, in fact, to leave a sizeable legacy when she died. Figuring out the details of that legacy would come soon enough—for now she had the opportunity to consider making investments in herself and her own personal joys. That opened up potentials she had never envisioned.

The diagonal lines are called your capital projection: it's your satiation spending calculated throughout your lifetime. As your chart comes together, it helps to articulate the sorts of plain-English questions and answers about your wealth that can be so hard to come by in this field. For instance:

1. *Increasing* your spending may decrease your prospective legacy but still provide reasonable assurance of securing your nut. That was absolutely the case for Mary.

2. *Reducing* spending may provide greater assurance of securing your nut (or a larger legacy). That comfort may be more important than some of your current expenses.

Of course there are more options than that. Adjusting your financial exposure (revisiting your financial snapshot and minimizing expenses while increasing projected income or returns) can raise the top line, which is your projected net worth. This was the case for Lance:

❖ LANCE
Finds a Way to Raise the Roof

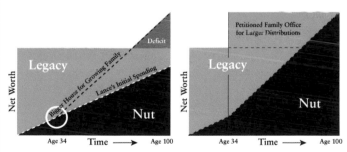

Lance and his wife had aspirations for adopting several children from countries they'd visited in their travels together. That idea ushered in a flood of questions: could they afford a larger house? Would his children be sufficiently provided for if an accident were to take Lance's life prematurely? What were the key timelines in his children's lives to make sure they maximized their own benefits from the family's wealth?

Starting with the question of a new home, initial calculations suggested that Lance's first choice was actually outside his means, even if he were to receive increased distributions from the family office. So he refined his hunt and found a house that was still a dramatic step up, both in size and comfort, for his growing family without breaking the bank.

The next hurdle was to approach the family office for the additional monthly distributions he would require to cover the mortgage on this new house. He was successful in his pitch—but that's another story. Stay tuned.

If your capital projection leaves a deficit (or doesn't leave enough of a legacy) all the way past your lifespan, you have two directions to consider. Go ahead, be enthusiastic and do both: 1) find new sources of wealth, as through paid work or refined strategies for managing what you already have, or 2) postpone or eliminate some of the things included in your satiation spending. If you choose the latter, search for the things that can wait; things that are outweighed by the peace of mind that comes with a secure nut.

Once your capital projection shows you are on track to secure your nut through the end of your projected lifespan, congratulations: Any excess becomes your legacy, often viewed as a whole separate portfolio altogether. Like the diagrams on the previous pages, your own projection will be an extreme simplification of your circumstances, but it does help determine what is most important in your life and whether you've got the resources to protect it. Assuring your nut gives you the unique opportunity to imagine.

- *Imagine* feeling secure about providing for your own needs—and those of your loved ones.
- *Imagine* no monetary restrictions on your life. Is there anything you'd like to try that you've never seriously considered?
- *Imagine* the freedom to refine and redirect your wealth plan. What if you could put your money into action in more meaningful ways?
- *Imagine* legacies that carry your ideals to future generations. What message would you send into the future?

There's so much focus on *burden* in life, on the things that are in our way or bogging us down. If life is a balancing act between burdens and potential, it's high time to load up the other side of the scale and seize those potentials of yours. This is the time I encourage all inheritors to stack up their dreams. Let your imagination soar—and all you doggedly practical types can trust that soon enough we'll come back to earth to start on the blueprints for your favorite wacky ideas.

If you must, start small: Imagine never clipping another coupon. Imagine giving bigger gifts to your loved ones and to the charities you respect. Imagine driving the car you want (instead of only what you think you can afford). Imagine flying first class some of the time—or *all* of the time.

Once you can imagine it, you can get a little more practical and see if you really want to put these ideas into action. If you want a fully staffed vacation home instead of a timeshare, it's time to determine if your nut will still be reasonably secure. Walk that line between joy and prudence and you may be amazed how often you can keep pushing the line deeper in the direction of joy without losing your foothold in prudence. You might even be surprised how prudence can bring its own joy.

❀ MARY...
Can Now Afford to Chase Her Dreams

Once she realized her nut was secure (and thus she could reasonably expect to support all of her needs and desires for a lifetime), Mary began to pursue the question of "What now?" She loved her career as a social worker, but frankly was getting older and more fatigued with the stress and pressures of the job. When she attended a wealth seminar in her late 50s, she allowed herself, for the first time that she could remember, to consider what other life passions she might want to pursue.

As a child, she'd spent her happiest hours at her

grandmother's ranch caring for all the animals—but with a special fondness for the horses. Her eyes still sparkle when she describes the life lessons she learned in the saddle.

She began to look into the work (and finances) of buying and running a horse ranch. With wealth coaching and the help of the family's accountants, she determined that she had the means to buy a horse property outside Chicago and hire the staff she would need to oversee the ranch's operation.

Often the work to pursue your dreams calls on the others on your wealth team as much as it requires your own persistence. In Lance's case, though he walked into the family office all alone, he made sure to enlist the support of team members he could trust to prepare himself.

✿ LANCE
Petitions the Family Office

When it came time to approach his family office for the higher monthly distributions he needed to afford his new house, Lance had done his homework. He knew the office would only speak to him in private, so he took pains to review all the details he and I could assemble on the nature of his family trusts and his ability to access them. Together we estimated his needs (through nut calculations) and finally role-played the skills and knowledge he would need for this face-to-face encounter.

These preparations paid off with a surprisingly quick (and unprecedented) OK from the family office. Lance began receiving almost five times his previous monthly distributions, allowing him ample resources to upgrade houses and employ the nanny and domestic help that would maximize his own free time.

At your level of inheritance, you can begin to look at how you will invest your energy as well as your money throughout your lifetime. Frankly, for anyone at any stage of relations with their wealth, energy is the more precious commodity. It's tempting, when looking at balance sheets, financial snapshots, satiation spending calculations, and a capital projection to secure your nut, to get caught up in the quantitative: "What can I afford?" Good question, but first ask it like this: "What can I afford to expend my *energy* on? Where do I *want* to invest my time and attention?"

When you want to use energy toward something, it's no longer spending; it's investing, it's engaging your passions. That's a different (and deeper) wishing well than financial fortune, no matter how large the fortune. You tap into wants, dreams, and goals, then you link up your financial resources to these same passions and whoa Nelly, you're gonna go places.

Life's Too Short: Down with Drudgery

The wisdom of life consists in the elimination of
non-essentials. Besides the noble art of getting things
done, there is a nobler art of leaving things undone.
LIN YUTANG, CHINESE AUTHOR AND INVENTOR

Planning for more than one lifetime begins with getting that first lifetime (yours) squared away. The nut did that from a financial standpoint, but just because that capital projection rises steadily and confidently up and to the right without poking through the top, it doesn't do it alone. Here's where you employ your wealth management team to help keep those lines where they belong. By this point you've done the hard work—establishing your starting point and projecting a course for your lifetime. Now you can pass on this information to a trusted advisor who can keep tabs on your progress. Together, you'll adjust and adapt your plans at various stages in the future.

Your satiation spending and your plan for securing your nut are the foundations for your personal business plan. This business plan—which forms the basis of your life's vision and mission statement—becomes a set of marching orders for your wealth management team. In one respect, oversimplified of course, from here on out much of the work is monitoring and maintenance. Even the parts of your plan that must be created from scratch now have a mission statement; that is more than most advisors receive from their clients.

There are other charts, other lines, you should be tracking in your life; call one the happiness or fulfillment chart. You should go through a similar process, focusing on your personal energy, setting "satiation spending" of how you want to engage your energy on a daily basis, and eventually assuring that the "nut" of your personal lifelong fulfillment is assured, according to projections. That *happiness projection line,* traveling up and to the right, also needs help if you have even a modicum of personal ambition. In the same way that your wealth team can manage many, if not virtually all, details of your financial future, daily life is filled with tasks that can eat up your free time and divert you from your ultimate callings. Remember, this book is about seizing your potential to enrich your own future. How can you be future-oriented if you are too busy *now* to explore your calling?

There *are* chores that keep each one of us grounded in a good way. Dishes, sorting recycling, alphabetizing ties by color—everyone has some obsessive compulsion that somehow balances out all the rest of the ways that we're perfectly sensible in our lives. I don't know many people who would genuinely be happy in the role of a Caesar, reclining among servants and being fed grapes all day. For one thing you really should get more exercise and have a better diet than that. For another thing, all those Caesars always seemed to come to a violent and ugly end. Let's save the beheadings and back-stabbings for someone else, shall we?

On your various to-do lists, there are chores that can be categorized along this spectrum.

1. **I MUST.** At the top are those that are impractical to delegate, somehow your own personal albatrosses. OK, fair enough. You didn't think I was going to wipe clean your *whole* to-do list, did you? Honestly, some of these things are good. Articulating your life vision, taking care of yourself, brushing your teeth ... Don't forget that some of your "musts" are actually healthy for you; some of them feed your soul. When you really investigate why you do some of the things you do, you may find hobbies, pastimes, and activities that you simply can't do without.

2. **I LIKE.** Some things you actually like to do. It's good to see the distinction that you're *choosing* to do these things, and yet if something more pressing were to come up, you technically could delegate them when needed.

3. **I DISLIKE.** Let's face it, life's messier than all these little neat charts we make. We certainly get stuck with duties we don't like, and sometimes we have to soldier through. You can get mad about it, or you can simply get 'em done and move on to better things. There are

very few things, however, that *can't* be delegated in this life, so put your dislikes high on your list of things you'd love to turn loose to someone else.

4. I CAN'T or I WON'T! These are the easy ones to identify, but not always the easiest to discard. Your very attitude toward them (and it's a *bad* attitude, I can tell already) can make these hard to delegate. You went to the trouble to rate these at the very bottom of the list; I'm sensing some resentment here. (Would you like to talk about it?)

The important revelations of this exercise are threefold: 1) Not everything on your to-do list is a chore—you might even *like* some of your tasks. 2) All except the "I Musts" *can* be delegated; and thus 3) whatever you continue doing, you *choose* to do. Vent those "Can't/Won't" frustrations to your therapist, your wealth coach, or this very page (no violence, please). And then bask in your newfound peace with the three revelations above. A personal mentor, someone like a life coach, can help you sort

> *When managed well, your great potential overpowers the risks.*

through some of the stickiest details here. You're not the first one to list those items under "Can't/Won't," and for everyone who's ever listed them there are at least a half dozen companies named ACME or AAAardvark in the phone book or conveniently listed on the Web who will gladly do them for a small fee.

The Substance of Dreams (Inheritors Can Fly, Too)

Life is definitely not all drudgery, and now that you have some ideas for clearing away some of the unpleasant tasks, perhaps you have a little more capacity for pondering your higher callings.

I'm not sure where or when it happened, but somewhere along the way people with significant fortunes became convinced that it was a ton of work to be rich. Warren Miller, the ski-movie maker, was probably borrowing from Gandhi or Confucius or someone when he said, "It's expensive to be rich." This book's cover artwork provides a nice illustration of the simple point that every inheritance comes with costs and with risks. But the point of the book's title is that when managed well, your great potential overpowers those risks. In other words, if you weather the struggle to understand your financial position, if you then articulate and pursue a vision for your future, then your efforts pay off in the greatest way possible: You enrich your life and you seize your potential. *Carpe potentia!*

Remember the "miracle of compound interest" snowball effect mentioned back in Chapter 5? It works for human potential, too. Go after your aspirations: build the skills, assemble your team, develop the experience to understand life's complexities, chart a course through your own personal dreams.

As you achieve each benchmark on your path, you set ever-greater goals, like tracing a dot-to-dot path to the stars.

Don't get too far ahead of yourself; remember the parable of "with one eye fixed on your destination there is only one eye left with which to find the way." Now is a great time, however, to make sure you've not only shed the burdens you can delegate, but that you're also taking on the dreams and challenges that you've always imagined.

I'm keeping this discussion deliberately vague. I certainly have my own personal favorite dreams, but I won't presume to tell you the sorts of butterflies you should be chasing in your life. I've known inheritors who wanted to race cars, raise children, win Olympic medals, or start global charities. I've known some who just wanted enough quiet time each day to meditate or read a book and sip tea. I've known one who wanted to travel to the moon. Everyone has potential on this planet, including you. You're special in that you have exceptional means and resources to achieve that potential, and to discover and achieve further potentials above and beyond. One area that might resonate for you, though, is the world of philanthropy.

Philanthropy: The Wealth of Giving

The true meaning of life, Wesley, is to plant trees under whose shade you do not expect to sit.
NELSON HENDERSON, FATHER OF WESLEY

To me, philanthropy is more about giving *back* than it is about giving into. When you give into, you are responding to outside pressures (of a board? or friends? or the media?). Giving *back* comes from within: Its foundation is appreciation.

❦ MARY
A New Angle Bridges Her Two Lives

Now in her 70s, Mary runs her Illinois horse ranch with a clearly personal touch. She rides the fence lines side by side with the young ranch hands and chats amiably with the boarders who keep their horses at her ranch. This passion bridges the Mary of today with the little girl within her who grew up loving horses. Horseback riding, in fact, was her first refuge as a child when she'd suffered abuse within her own family. After turning to her grandmother's horses, she'd gone into social work.

Visiting a casual reunion of her old social-worker colleagues a few years back, Mary had the idea to introduce abused children to the therapeutic side of horseback riding. She's currently establishing a foundation that will allow inner-city victims of child abuse to spend a week at her ranch, learning the power, grace, and confidence that Mary herself has always received from working with horses. Rather than marking a dividing point in her life, her wealth has become a point of connection, to her own potential and to the potentials of others.

One example of the sometimes counterintuitive principles at work when managing inheritors' larger portfolios is the value of philanthropy. How can giving money away add to your wealth? The raw tax benefits of charitable giving are an obvious and oft-touted benefit: "Give your money to charity, not the IRS." But it can be more inspiring than that. Support (or even create) organizations that endorse your values, ones that address the

Life's out there waiting to be lived, and your wealth is awaiting direction.

problems that concern you most, and you're investing in a shared future. Put your money to work toward making a better world, one where your style of investing (and living) is more richly rewarded, and you're grasping the principles of multigenerational thinking.

I hear this a lot: "I feel hollow when I write checks to charity." Or, "Maybe if I write a large check they'll leave me alone." (Dream on!) Or, "I haven't figured out yet what I want to support." Like trying to get romance all figured out before you fall in love, we're all guilty, at some time or another, of procrastinating or sidestepping the decisions facing us. Life's out there waiting to be lived, and your wealth is awaiting direction. The same principle applies to philanthropy. Spend your whole life, or even most of your time for a whole year, trying to find the "best charity" or the "most worthy cause" and you'll probably find yourself ultimately going backwards. The world is spinning fast beneath us; get some plans up to speed or it will pass you by. If in doubt, start, like Mary, by searching within yourself. What do you appreciate?

Chasing something as seemingly vague as your own passions and joys may seem like chasing butterflies into an unknown forest. If not, humor me. Life's most memorable experiences come from venturing into the unknown. And if you're going to make a habit (or a sizeable investment) of venturing into the unknown, it can be nice to have a guide. When you find kindred spirits, people you trust doing things you admire, then let them be a contagion. The key is that dialogue between you (your passions and intentions) and them. You don't have to figure out solutions to all the world's problems, but you should imbue your money with *your* intentions before you send it on a mission.

It doesn't take a family fortune to direct dollars into the world with the power of your commitments and integrity … Each of us, as individuals, gives money this generative power when we make even the most routine choices with intention. We can consciously put money in the hands of projects, programs, companies, and vendors we respect and trust, and even approach paying taxes as a way of expressing our commitment and investment as citizens.
LYNNE TWIST, *SOUL OF MONEY*

Whether you participate in philanthropy or not, the key is a larger view—one that is not merely reactionary to current circumstances or pressures. Your special potential as an inheritor is that you have the opportunity to look beyond the necessities of everyday life and find something deeper, more lasting, and intimately personal to you and only you.

And so, in the interest of turning you loose to seize those potentials, I shall endeavor to bring this book to maturity. Call forth the final chapter.

CHAPTER SEVEN

Inheritance for Life
(Seizing Your Potential)

*If hard work were such a wonderful thing,
surely the rich would have kept it all to themselves.*
LANE KIRKLAND, LABOR UNION LEADER

Work Smarter, Not Harder

Being an inheritor is a lot of work toward some pretty amazing possibilities. Would you rather be burdened with potential or free to pursue mediocrity? There I go again, overdramatizing the situation. Naturally, non-inheritors aren't all mediocre, but they don't have something you do. And it's not just money. As you've learned by now (or already knew and are thanking me for only harping on it one more time), wealth is more than financial. Inheritance is about passing on values, dreams, and stories—and it's about finding the freedom to create and nurture *your own* values, dreams, and stories.

Perhaps by now you agree that there's enough to do—both right away and throughout your life—that you need a reliable team to share the work. But you understand (or at least you're nodding your head and faking it well) that delegation doesn't take you out of the picture. In fact, done right, delegation lifts you to greater responsibilities on your team: You manage your managers and orchestrate your wealth plans from the highest level.

✵ LANCE

Lists of "Someday, Maybe" vs. "In My Life, For Sure"

Over time, Lance's focus has evolved with his lifestyle. In his 20s, he aspired to race sailboats but never seriously pursued it, thinking his access to his distributions from the family office was fixed and nonnegotiable. In his 30s, he did some work abroad, within the means of his distributions, and decided to get married, which precipitated deeper understanding of his ability to access his funds. He didn't comply with the family office's standard "prenup," which was perhaps the first step he had taken toward independence—and the family office was none too pleased!

Upon his decision to adopt and raise several children, Lance gained the knowledge and confidence to approach the family office for increased access to his funds, allowing him to upgrade homes, live abroad for a year with his family, and pay for the help he needed to stay focused on his greatest passions.

Now in his 40s, Lance is preparing for the second half of his life. His family office has informed him that tax laws favor paying tuition, so he doesn't have to worry about all his children's education—not now or ever. The same holds for all his family's medical expenses. He has taken care of his wife's needs, in case something should happen to him, so that she will have sufficient funds for a lifetime. And now he's beginning to address the idea of an ongoing legacy.

Lance has established remarkable degrees of control over his own wealth—especially in the face of a stingy, draconian family office. While he's a quick learner and a hands-on guy, he has learned that there is far more to the day-to-day management of his wealth than he can personally tackle. So he has assembled a team of experts he trusts, from a wealth coach and personal attorneys (who hold his own interests above their own) to domestic help that can shoulder the daily routines.

He doesn't have unlimited time to pursue all the big ideas that he dreams of, but every year he seems to take a firm step further out of life's burdens and into the realm of his potentials as a human being.

Operating at that level, much like a chief executive at a corporation, requires learning a whole different set of knowledge, skills, and coping mechanisms. The best corporate execs won't fly solo through it all, they know their own energy and time is as valuable an asset as their ability to work long hours. A little wise delegation and collaborative teamwork is always far more effective than the lonesome and foolish attempt to solve every problem single-handedly.

So the old axiom "work smarter, not harder" comes to play here. The great part is that it's not all about your own smarts. Someone smarter than I am once said that you don't have to know all the answers; you just have to know where to look.[9] When you find yourself drifting astray, a little confidence in your own abilities to ask good questions, patiently pursue elusive answers, and redirect your course is really all that's called for here.

You miss 100 percent of the shots you don't take.
WAYNE GRETZKY, HOCKEY GREAT

I think this is a great time to remind yourself that it's OK to take shots and it's OK to miss some of them. You can't do everything yourself, and you and your team aren't always going to get it right. Give yourself permission to stumble, bumble, and fail—and trust in your fellow teammates to help pick you up and dust you off. You might also expect

---

[9] It was Einstein, and I found that out by knowing where to look.

to do the same for the professionals who serve you—that is unless you found them listed under "perfect people" in the phone book.

❦ ALYSA
Learns a Good Leader Is Never Alone

There were times, in all those years getting her arms around Yia Yia's real estate holdings and stock portfolio, when Alysa just wanted to turn it all over to someone else and get back to her old life. But the more items she checked off her financial to-do list, the more she realized that managing the details of this sort of wealth could be easier than she first thought. It came down to the principle of *work smarter, not harder.*

She still relies heavily on wealth coaching to guide her toward each next step and the skills she will need at new stages of the process. Unlike Lance, Alysa is not the sort of inheritor who intends to function as a sort of CEO of her wealth plan. But by enlisting a core group of trusted experts and intelligently delegating appropriate tasks to each of them, she is able to stay abreast of her plan's progress.

The confidence and sense of initiative that have grown from Alysa's involvement in her family's partnership have translated to other areas of her life. Over time, she responded to the challenge she had heard in coaching sessions: to find her own true passions and engage her time and energy (and money, if needed) toward them. As an indication of her gaining momentum, she has just formed a band, plans to open a recording studio, and will soon be sharing her guitar passion with fellow musicians and live audiences.

Admittedly, there are plenty of specific skills to develop. Learn the basics of finance by taking a continuing education course or a one-day seminar from a local college or organization. Participate in one of those weekend seminars with handsome, well-spoken inspirational types. Read recommended books on the subject (try my suggestions, following this chapter). Schedule a session with a wealth coach or other knowledgeable expert whose style syncs nicely with your own.

And *keep* learning. Every few years get an update on the wealth management theories that have come into vogue. Read (or skim) your financial groups' newsletters. If you trust their work, test their ability to sort through all the daily headlines: hopefully they share only the relevant news. Subscribe to blogs from experts who write about your type of circumstances. We're thinking and planning for a long time, so the learning is never done. Participate eagerly in the unfolding of history as if you were a perpetual student of life.

Things Change: Charge Boldly into the Unknown

Let's say you're one heck of a student of life and you feel like you've got it all figured out. Most people like surprises, at least the nice ones, and I'm convinced they're part of the mix in a healthy life. A sure way to build surprise into your life is to try new things, venture into the unknown, and—on occasion—wing it. Not sure how to wing it? No worries. No matter how ironclad your plans seem to be, just when you've got it all figured out, life has a way of throwing a wrench in your plans. Life's good like that.

If you leave trust assets to your spouse, how do you define *spouse*? Sounds simple till you consider the possibility of remarriage, same-sex marriage (which may not be recognized by certain governing authorities), and common-law marriage. And it gets downright muddy when multiple trustees and attorneys with different jurisdictions come into the picture. Even saying, "I want my money to go to my children" is not specific enough for this level of wealth conservation. Which children and in what amounts? Have you considered the prospects of divorces, stepchildren, and adoptions in your family? At what age and with what caveats will your beneficiaries receive their benefits? What if tax laws change and the red tape, legal fees, and management costs outweigh the "gift" you think you're providing? What if the trustee of your funds breaks your trust and squanders the money or unfairly withholds it from your children? What if you survive your own children? What if you're an income beneficiary of a trust that terminates at your death, and the corpus (property held in trust) would go to your children—but you don't have any children?

Many of the questions are tough ones. If you don't answer them, trust me, someone you don't know might do it for you. Whatever they are, I like your answers better than those of a bureaucrat interpreting legalese for you. Though the questions are difficult, taking them on is a responsibility of wealth. Welcome to planning for more than one lifetime.

On the financial side, you'll want regular updates from your experts. The status of your taxes, both annually and quarterly, is a given (or will be once you insist), but depending on what you own and operate as part of your estate, you may also have quarterly estimated taxes due, annual Crummey[10] letters to beneficiaries, family business financials to study before board or shareholder meetings, site visits to complete for allocating grants, and so on and so on until you need a bigger calendar.

Taxes are just one aspect of your financial picture to update regularly. I might even argue they should occupy the least of your time and energy. After all, taxes are essentially the art of complying with a set of rules which can and do change. The trickier—and thus more interesting and worthy of your wits—issues are in managing complex assets like

---

[10] For once I'm not being saucy here. They're really called that, after an individual who went after the IRS and won the right to—well, it's complicated, but let's just say Mr. Crummey did many inheritors a favor. By writing these letters once a year, certain types of inheritors qualify for some tax-free gift exclusions.

rental properties, partnerships, family-owned (privately-held) operating companies, or questions of your legacy.

For your corporate assets, tune into annual reports, board of director meetings, and other indications of how business is progressing. For your properties, expect (and require) regular status reports on occupancy, taxes, marketing, and other indicators of profitability and business health. And for your legacy, well, let's spend a whole paragraph on that one, shall we?

> *I think of a legacy not as a dot on a landscape or an X on a treasure map, but as an arrow. It's a direction, not a destination.*

Your *legacy* encompasses everything you set in motion while you're alive. That's a pretty broad lens, but it provides a perspective that I highly recommend. From business ventures, family units, and charitable efforts to the estate you intend to leave to your beneficiaries, it even includes your hobbies, the things you create, and all that you want to share of yourself. That's a lot of stuff that hopefully is all connected through a common thread—your values and your dreams.

I think of a legacy not as a dot on a landscape or an X on a treasure map, but as an arrow. It's a direction, not a destination. And as you go through life, even from day to day, that arrow might point in slightly different directions. It might even point in *opposite* directions at various times.

All who wander are not lost. A path that doubles back or loops around may actually be the fastest way around some of the boulders, mountains, or canyons that life puts in the middle of our respective journeys.

❀ **MARY**
  What 200 Children Might Someday Think of Her
    Childless in a family whose wealth has no further generations of blood relatives to benefit, Mary has found a larger life for her money, both while she's here and once she's gone. Do the math: If 50 abused children benefit from a week at Mary's ranch, and they share the benefits of that experience with their own children and so on, within three generations Mary's efforts will have touched several hundred lives. That sort of solution may not work for every inheritor, but it sure resonates with Mary to this very day.

    Personally, I've witnessed a transformation in Mary, from the sheepish downward gaze of the inheritor living a double life to the confident composure of a woman who has embraced her wealth as her own and has begun to put it to work in service of her own visions.

A Zen riddle asks, "How do you travel a road of 99 curves while going straight?" In certain odd sects of Zen you will be hit with a cane for any answer whatsoever that you offer. It's a strange (and violent) approach, but one takeaway is worthwhile: You don't travel that road at all by sitting there answering silly riddles. Nike actually summed it up more succinctly and managed to sell a few hundred million shoes in the process: "Just Do It."

You're Not Done Yet!

Bonus points for getting to the final section of the final chapter in this book. There's something satisfying about finishing a book, setting it down, and saying to yourself, "Well *there's* another thing to check off my to-do list." I don't want to take anything away from that–take that sense of satisfaction with my compliments. Hopefully I have shared some thoughts that stick somewhere behind your eyeballs. Here's one that may not sit so quietly and prettily: You're not done yet. You will *never* be done.

The challenge of seizing your potential is one of life's ultimate false summits. Step one: Get a handle on what your inheritance is—how much money you have and what baggage is attached. Most people *without* money think that summit is the top of the mountain. Once you realize you have enough to never require paid work, well, it's all downhill from there, right? *Wrong.*

When you've grasped the financial reality of your wealth, it's time to start ascending the mountain of emotional realities. This stage of the journey begins with the history of your wealth, its story, the values it carries, and the connection it creates with those who have come before you. Next is the present, who you are now, at the crossroads of your own past and future (and those of your wealth). And finally you approach this particular summit by reconfirming (or redirecting) the arrow of your aspirations—the future of your life and your legacy. And from that lofty vantage point you will see—

another, higher summit.

Never climbed a mountain? They often work like that. It's a trick of visual perspective. We are only so many feet tall: Stand on the side of a mountain, below a hump that's not actually the top, and the mountain itself obscures its own summit. You see a nice pointy top up there. You climb and climb and tell yourself you're almost there, and you do finally reach it, only to gain the new perspective that there is another, higher pitch to climb.

Me, I get headaches over 13,000 feet, so I'm not going to extend my false-summit analogy to the point where you get one, too. I believe the process of achieving your potential then seeing new and higher potentials is never ending. There is no top of this mountain and you can keep going higher every year. Thanks to life's ability to constantly surprise us, we need not even be confined to one analogy like that of a mere mountain. "Potential" like "legacy" is such a wonderfully broad, adaptable term that it can mean just about anything you might aspire to achieve. We can *always* be better at anything we do; it's too limiting to consider only sheer measurements of monetary worth. It's even limiting to think in terms of numbers of charities, children, or other beneficiaries you support. Numbers, like forms of money, are figments of our imagination. In the very first chapter of *The Soul of Money*, Lynne Twist calls money "a distinctly human invention."

Three other things that may seem like inventions or figments of our imagination are *values, dreams,* and *meaning.* But they are just too intuitive, too naturally occurring, too universal, and too unpredictable to be considered inventions. This trilogy is often relegated to the special home for ideas without substance —and yet they are, counterintuitively, the stuff of substance in a changing world. As the author of *Zen and the Art of Motorcycle Maintenance,* wrote:

> *Values are not the least vague when you're dealing with them in terms of actual experience. It is only when you bring back statements about them and try to integrate them into the overall jargon ... that they become vague.*
> ROBERT PIRSIG, *LILA*

Actual experience. Traveling that road of 99 curves. Making your values, your beliefs, your story, your dreams, your *wealth* something of substance. That is now your charge. Seize *this* potential and you will realize a new, brighter reality of inherited wealth: You will find yourself living richly.

Burden? Pshaw. Myths? Phooey. Go forth and enjoy your potential.

Further Resources

BOOKS

Legacy of Inherited Wealth: *Interviews with Heirs,*
edited by Barbara Blouin and Katherine Gibson, Trio Press
(The Inheritance Project, Inc.) 1995 [Revised 3rd Edition]

This book is a self-proclaimed "view from within" fea
turing 17 short stories from heirs in their own words. Their
stories speak for themselves; the only editorial commentary
appears in the introduction and afterword. That leaves it
to you, the reader, to draw your own conclusions. In my
opinion, the book's value is less about drawing conclusions
or receiving cautionary advice, but rather the demystifying
of inheritance's many challenges. If you're in the early stages
of understanding your inheritance, though—and especially
if you're feeling overwhelmed—this engaging book is a
first step to realizing you're not alone. Available only from
www.inheritance-project.com.

The Inheritor's Handbook: *A Definitive Guide for*
Beneficiaries, by Dan Rottenberg, Bloomberg 1999

Rottenberg brings a refreshingly direct approach to

the human side of inheritance: I like his ability to get right into practical tips and advice for inheritors. Admittedly, this book is for inheritors of any size fortune, so the upper tier of inheritors—those for whom paid work is purely optional—may prefer to skim certain sections of the book. The author himself encourages readers to skip to their most relevant section: Part 1 is for those whose benefactor is still alive (and thus you may have a say in the structure of your benefits). Part 2 is for those whose benefactor has just recently died. And Part 3 is for those who are already many years into dealing with their inheritance. This simple logical structure, along with the book's checklists, case studies, and hands-on exercises makes it a helpful workbook for the do-it-yourselfer.

The Inheritor's Sherpa, by Myra Salzer,
The Wealth Conservancy 2005

For those who longed to mark up this copy of *Living Richly* with colored pencils or red ink, my first book is more of a workbook, one that encourages you to engage in a series of exercises to home in on your own path toward sensible wealth management and a fulfilling life. When you have completed it, you will realize that at least half the story is your own.

Family Wealth—Keeping It in the Family: How Family Members and Their Advisers Preserve Human, Intellectual,

and Financial Assets for Generations, by James E. Hughes
Jr., Bloomberg 2004

This is, simply put, a watershed book in the field of
wealth management. I would like to make it required reading for every inheritor who is, or was, part of a family (yes,
that's all of them). I must admit, however, that this book
is highly involved stuff and frankly much of Hughes' focus
is on how *your advisors* should be conducting their jobs.
That said, if you're having issues with people on your wealth
management team, this book provides plenty of food for
thought. In an ideal world, I'd say: read it yourself, get your
advisors to read it, and then *discuss.*

Family: The Compact Among Generations,
by James E. Hughes Jr., Bloomberg 2007

If Hughes' first book leaned more toward advice for
advisors, this second book takes time to articulate the fundamental philosophies of his work. So, interestingly, you may
want to read it before its predecessor, *Family Wealth.* This is
good reading for inquiring inheritors who want models for
understanding the various roles of people they will encounter in managing their wealth (both its financial and human
components). As in his first book, Hughes' ultimate aim is
to help families overcome the phenomenon of "shirtsleeves-
to-shirtsleeves in three generations."

Preparing Heirs: *Five Steps to a Successful Transition of Family Wealth and Values,* by Roy Williams and Vic Preisser, RDR 2003

This is one of the leading studies that supported the ominous figure that 70 percent of all wealth transitions fail. Using data from 3,250 families, the researchers and coaches at the Williams Group quickly drew the conclusion that financial mechanics were hardly to blame for failed transfers of family wealth. Instead, it was the failure of families to communicate their values that doomed those transitions that failed. The book's first four chapters explain their study and analyze its resulting data, with some refreshingly personal anecdotes included throughout. Chapter 5 is the beginning of specific advice and guidance for families of wealth.

The Soul of Money: *Transforming Your Relationship with Money and Life,* by Lynne Twist, W.W. Norton & Co. 2003

Activist and global fundraiser Lynne Twist has put decades of achingly poignant life work on the pages of this book. It's an intense and inspiring read which spends a lot of time on the fundamental myths and misconceptions we hold about money. Unlike so many books that revel in tearing down myths, concluding with nothing more inspiring than "money is dirty," Twist's ultimate goal is to create a new ideology in which money is a vessel for our highest ideals. Certainly the book's primary goal is to refresh people's view of philanthropy but ultimately its lessons transcend money, challenging us to make a positive difference in the world—whatever form that difference might take.

Silver Spoon Kids: *How Successful Parents Raise Responsible Children,* by Eileen Gallo, Ph.D. and Jon Gallo, J.D., Contemporary Books 2002

By including a foreword written by their own son (nice touch), you have immediate assurance that this couple practices what they preach! I found this book rich in helpful advice and positive encouragement—both of which seem to be in short supply for parents today raising their children in a climate of affluence. Even more than its sequel (see below) this book is aimed at upper tiers of inheritors—those for whom paying work may not be necessary.

The Financially Intelligent Parent: *8 Steps To Raising Successful, Generous, Responsible Children,* by Eileen Gallo, Ph.D. and Jon Gallo, J.D., NAL Trade 2005

These two authors—a psychotherapist and an estate attorney—share both personal and professional experience in the issues of parenting children born into wealth. An engaging read for *any* parent, the book is clear in its intent: "We don't believe that money harms children, or adults either, for that matter. It's not the money that we should worry about; it's the money values we're teaching our kids!"

Children of Paradise: Successful Parenting for Prosperous Families, by Lee Hausner, Ph.D., Tarcher 1990

Primarily written for parents who are wealth creators (rather than heirs themselves), this book details the many pitfalls of raising children in affluence. Despite its title, it's really more a series of admonitions than a set of keys to successful childrearing. By the end of the book the author even acknowledges that readers may find themselves disheartened. If you're the type of reader who learns from such cautionary advice, you may find this a helpful background to common parenting pitfalls.

The Golden Ghetto: The Psychology of Affluence, by Jessie H. O'Neill, Hazelden 1997

At times bleak—the introduction contends "it is a rare and exceedingly well-balanced individual who can possess great material wealth and survive emotionally"—this book is valuable for those who want to probe the psychological underpinnings (and pitfalls) of inheritance. The author is, herself, an heir to part of a General Motors fortune and she shares abundant details of her own personal struggles throughout the book.

The Wise Inheritor: A Guide to Managing, Investing and Enjoying Your Inheritance, by Ann Perry, Broadway 2003

Written by the heir to a modest bequest gained from the game "Go Fish," this book's greatest offering is its first-person perspective on receiving an inheritance. Perry admits frankly, for instance, to struggling with the financially sensible but emotionally difficult prospects of selling off the family stock and properties that hold personal meaning for her. The author draws on her experience as a personal finance newspaper columnist, so her financial tips may be too general (or dated) for upper-level inheritors, whom the book calls "ultrarich." Read it for the human perspective of a fellow inheritor.

Wealth in Families, by Charles W. Collier,
Harvard University 2006

Written by the senior philanthropic adviser at Harvard, there is a strong altruistic angle to this book. Collier includes some intriguing interviews with the field's key thinkers, like Jay Hughes and Lee Hausner. Reading these may provide a succinct entree to these other writers' work and help you determine if you would like to read their own (longer) books.

FILM

Born Rich [film], directed by Jamie Johnson,
Wise and Good Films 2003

Heir to the Johnson & Johnson fortune, Jamie Johnson turns the camera on himself and his peers—a small group of young, ultra-rich heirs. The reviews of this film weren't exactly glowing, but it's worth an hour and a quarter to hear first hand some of the common issues and uncertainties plaguing inheritors at any level. Love or hate the personalities that appear on camera with their unpolished gripes and often snobby naïveté, the film does, at least, make a noble (if amateur) effort to bring the taboo subject of inherited wealth into mainstream discussion. If I sound more like a film critic than someone who works with inheritors, suffice it to say I have mixed emotions about this film. I longed for a more inspirational takeaway, but for inheritors just getting their arms around their situation, this is a quick way to realize "you're not alone" and "you've got at least as much going for you as these kids."

EVENTS & ORGANIZATIONS

Institute for Private Investors

[a private membership organization for wealthy families]

IPI provides education and networking for families who have substantial assets (and their advisors). IPI features a significant online community for these 1,100 investors as well as a number of events across the U.S. and abroad. All of the group's work is in a safe harbor: IPI *does not sell* advice, products, or a particular point of view—that's your assurance that this is neutral investor education. Learn more at <u>Memberlink.net</u>.

Inherited Wealth and You [a workshop I developed and co-facilitate with other professionals]

I host intensive hands-on workshops for inheritors, covering various topics related to wealth management, life balance, and planning for the future. I've found that bringing together inheritor peers is sometimes the fastest and most direct way to articulate and confront the challenges you face. Groups are small enough that we custom-tailor each event to specific needs and challenges. Upcoming events appear at TheWealthConservancy.com.

ARTICLES & OTHER RESOURCES

"Seven Secrets of the Purposeful Trust™*"* [articles],
by John A. Warnick, 2009

Warnick is the founder of Family Wealth Transitions and Solutions, a consulting firm that assists clients and their advisory teams in the areas of purposeful planning as well as trust design and implementation. He delivers workshops across the nation for estate planning attorneys and financial planners. To learn more, visit: johnawarnick.com.

EstateLogic® *from Executor's Resource* [software],
available at ExecutorsResource.com.

Full disclosure: this is a tool I helped develop for anyone—from individuals to advisors—to organize estate and legacy details. I would spread the love to other competing pieces of software, but frankly that's why I created a team to develop this one: I couldn't find anything else that was custom tailored to these particular needs. You might think of it sort of like a TurboTax® for estate settlement.

ADDITIONAL REFERENCES CITED

(p. 3) *A Joseph Campbell Companion: Reflections on the Art of Living* by Joseph Campbell, HarperCollins (New York), 1993

(p. 7) *Sudden Money: Managing a Financial Windfall*, by Susan Bradley, CFP with Mary Martin, PhD, John Wiley & Sons 2000 p. 19

(p. 110) "The Laws of the Earth and the Laws of Economics" [article], by Donella H. Meadows, founder of the Sustainability Institute. http://www.sustainer.org/?page_id=90&display_article=vn674economics%26earthed

(p. 112) *Instructing the Martial Arts,* by Charles Ralph Heck. McFarland & Co., Inc. 1988 p. 66

(p. 159) *Lila: An Inquiry into Morals*, by Robert M. Pirsig, Bantam 1991 p. 67

ABOUT THE AUTHOR

Regularly listed among the country's top financial advisors by *Worth* magazine, Myra Salzer is the founder and president of The Wealth Conservancy, Inc. After founding the firm in 1983, Salzer began specializing in fee-only financial planning as a wealth coach and inheritor's advocate. Her specialty is "interior finance," or the personal aspects of inherited wealth.

She published *The Inheritor's Sherpa: A Life-Summiting Guide for Inheritors* in 2005. In 2008, she developed TIES (The Inheritor's Empowerment System), a series of nine steps for inheritors who want to harness the potentials of their wealth and realize their greatest life ambitions.

A member of the National Association of Personal Financial Advisors (NAPFA), Salzer is a frequent speaker at conferences in the field of financial services. She has been profiled and consulted in several financial journals and she co-facilitates periodic workshops to help inheritors engage their wealth toward their personal potential.

Before entering the financial services industry, Salzer earned a degree in chemical engineering and worked for major corporations in that field. She later became a CERTIFIED FINANCIAL PLANNER™ professional. She also founded a software company, Executor's Resource, to provide estate management and settlement products to executors and other financial advisors. For advancements in the software industry, particularly the development of

EstateLogic, Salzer was named *Financial Planning Magazine's* "Technology Wizard" in their 2010 Innovator Awards. Salzer has two grown daughters and lives in the foothills of the Rocky Mountains with her husband and dogs. Salzer can be reached through her firm's website, TheWealthConservancy.com.